Other Schiffer Books on Related Subjects:

Identifying Sarah Coventry Jewelry, 1949-2009
978-0-7643-4214-1, $39.99

Designed by RoS
Type set in Helvetica Neue/Archer

ISBN: 978-0-7643-4516-6
Printed in China

Published by Schiffer Publishing, Ltd.
4880 Lower Valley Road
Atglen, PA 19310
Phone: (610) 593-1777; Fax: (610) 593-2002
E-mail: Info@schifferbooks.com

Contents

Intro-
duction

> " *Her face he praises, but he courts her Ears.*
> *Catching the glitt'ring Pendants that she wears.* "
>
> ~ Sir Charles Sedley, *The Happy Pair*

*L*et's raid the jewelry boxes of the prestigious and the more representative women of history and see what earrings they wore. This book follows earrings through many incarnations, mostly from Europe and America, and through the wearers and the wearing. The authors have based it on reading history, asking questions of experts, and engaging in dialog with women whose earrings are part of their identities. It tells the big story of these small bijoux.

Fashion terms earrings as "extras," or accessories, but, for a woman, the type of earrings she wears is a signature of her attire, and many a woman feels naked without her earrings.

There is sometimes a prejudice regarding women who love jewelry. Perhaps people think it compensates for something, yet the love of adornment has a natural basis. Over time, pieces of jewelry accrue symbolic coinage from the provenance, purchase, and hour when they were worn. It is impractical to wear antique clothes, but a woman can wear jewelry from a long-vanished era. Having on earrings invites attention to the frame of one's face, thus to the face itself, with a decorative note, a sparkle.

Earrings signal that the person is not so shy...that she is worthy of admiration and a second look. They exhibit a subtle hint about someone's life view. In the history of the Western world, some wear earrings and some don't; as a finishing touch, earrings are elective and personal.

The story of earrings is revealing about people. Jane Stanford sold her personal jewelry to benefit Stanford University, yet we see her array of earrings in a big painting because she wanted the jewelry memorialized. Barbara Hutton wished to take care of her fabulous pearl set. When a visitor wanted to see it, she answered, "The goose has it." Hutton had been told that pearls swallowed by a goose gain luster.

From ancient times, earrings have been intertwined with many aspects of culture: clothing and hair styles, the availability and trade of precious metals and gems, views of luxury and sensuality, types of lighting, sumptuary laws, the position of women, and the frivolities of the ruling class. However, like other jewelry, earrings' precious metals have been recycled to fund wars while gems were traded for necessities and freedom from servitude.

Whereas the history of fashion was once viewed primarily in terms of outfitting actors for the theater, now museums preserve and exhibit costumes. These exhibitions are often among the best-attended, like the retrospective of the English designer Alexander McQueen at the Metropolitan Museum in New York in 2011, among the ten most-visited shows in the museum's history. Meanwhile, the study of earrings is more like chasing a live quarry than something inanimate. Styles evolve and vanish, only to re-emerge when skillfully done with new life, as well as a new twist.

In the Western civilization, where individualism is valued, people like to be identified with the group, but shun something that becomes too prevalent. Moreover, fashion and personal style change; so does taste in earrings. With the years, our selection from the jewelry box alters, until we look at some earrings that used to be staples and realize we have been pushing them into the corner where they only take up space. Perhaps these now go into a dress-up box like the kind our mothers made for us.

However, the collector's taste evolves along a different path, of looking at rather than reflecting self. A collector's taste elevates and narrows, and then may broaden to more eclectic again. A person could end up with one single camellia bush or one butterfly in a glass case.

My appreciation of Persian carpets led to my love of earrings. Before I pushed aside a jeweled curtain to learn about earrings, I penetrated Tehran's great bazaar of Persian carpets and formed my taste by looking and learning. As an exchange student in Iran, I had just $100 of spending money for the summer. Habib, the father of the host family, took me shopping to the extraordinary stores deep in the arcades of the bazaar. From the piles of carpets shimmering in the penumbral light, I chose one whose pink and blue pastel flowers on a beige background were on the order of a bath rug. Habib was volubly upset: I had seen hundreds of fine carpets yet selected this one — he would have paid the difference for me to purchase a rug of quality. What would my family in America think?

Persian music, art, and language fascinated me, so I moved to Tehran six years later. Chris went there also, for his studies. Iran's capital had transitioned from a provincial place to a fast-paced international hub. Formerly people, even those with fine homes, had, on hot nights, slept on cots by the streams that flowed along the streets, where sheep had been herded, and sometimes packs of camels. A new, desert city, Tehran had little greenery or public parks then and high yellowish concrete walls hid residences that were very fine if you were inside to see them. During the evening, Tehranis piled into cars and went to Shemiran, north of the city, where they promenaded, enjoyed sherbets and kabobs from street sellers, and basked in the colored lights strung up with abundance.

Strange for the city that had, under the National Bank, the most extraordinary collection of jewels in the world — a sea of color and light — these strings of lights in Shemiran were the respite we sought. Also because of the color, Chris and I gravitated to the carpet seller's street, and had tea, pistachios, and cake on a stack of carpets. The fabulous trove of gems at the National Bank was overpowering, but the carpets were like jewels. Gradually, like lifting weights at a gym, we refined our taste: sometimes a threadbare ancient tribal was most beautiful of all. Meanwhile, from hearing the slap of the carpet seller's assistant turning over carpets, or examining knots on the underside, the aesthetic experience became imprinted on us. As Francis Haskin writes in *Rediscoveries in Art*: "Taste, however capricious, always depends on more than taste."

Until late in the twentieth century, in our society, men bought jewelry for women. Some years after living in Iran, I moved to Paris, where I totally reversed my understanding of how a woman comes by jewelry: I bought earrings for myself! The French make the distinction between jewelry of great material value, *la jouaillerie*, and costume jewelry, *les bijoux*. They also have a useful phrase for jewelry — *importante* — which seems self-explanatory, but whose meaning is about commanding a special place in your adornment rather than having value per se. To buy "important" items of jewelry, to prioritize that in one's wardrobe, is a bold step.

I was lucky to find a job in Paris that paid a good salary. Touring the city, I was like a lizard taking on camouflage. Every time I went out, I dressed chic. On long lunch breaks from the research institute, co-workers and I went to fashion shows, tried new restaurants, and, with my co-worker Catherine, I went on a quest to identify our signature perfumes (we decided on Shalimar and Joy). I went to every museum in Paris (except the dental museum) and attended most nights operas, ballets, movies, and concerts. Swirling quite carefree in culture and fun, I became drawn to earrings like a crow to a piece of silver foil. I consciously wanted to develop my sense of beauty as I had for carpets — and my pursuit became the earrings I saw in paintings, museums, fairs, expositions, and shops.

I can't possibly tell you how good it was to have active work in a research institute, to forget my doctoral studies, and have a great urban space be my university. There was so much to learn by wandering Paris, gaining direction in my life while not having, conversely, a clear sense of it. The dealers were welcoming — I was flattered when one offered me a job as shop girl — and there were long walks in the Marche aux Puces or outskirts of Paris to outdoor fairs and municipal museums. One evening I was browsing in a shop when a very elderly Russian woman was deciding which of the jewelry she had pawned long ago to buy back. She left a little pair of earrings that I bought, an anonymous heirloom of green and pink stones and tiny *en tremblant* enamel pendants that I treasure to this day.

Playing earring detective, I would detect a whisper of pearl or pendant in a portrait, which might well not show up in a reproduction. During this time, I bought antique earrings to wear, but also, in an ephemeral phase of my life, gazed at these miniature sculptures and sentinels to great traditions of artistry. Later I would crochet earrings and have a sense of what it's like to work in miniature. When I look in my jewelry box, which is filled with earrings of many eras and styles, it's like going to a museum of decorative arts.

When Chris and I were the parents of young children living in a dilapidated Victorian house in Westchester County, New York, and way over our heads with the mortgage, we decided to sell my earrings. He took them to Christie's and was told my earrings weren't going to get a reserve that made auctioning worthwhile. We sold my set of Cabinet des Fees, circa 1700, purchased from the daughter of Surrealist poet Paul Eluard's, and bought the washer and dryer our young family needed. Fortunately, I still have many of the earrings. It is magical from time to time to take them out and lay them down in a good light — a goddess's playthings — and recollect.

In my Paris collecting, I kept a sketchbook of the earrings that caught my interest and, in more detail, the pairs of earrings I purchased, front and back. My ambition was to have one of each of the most distinctive styles of the nineteenth century. Later I collected more eclectically. I especially enjoy seeing how women dress up in earrings, even if the jewelry is lacking distinction as objects. A woman who is confident in her look often completes her person by adorning her ears. One day I was waiting with my daughter for a cappuccino at the bookstore and complimented the woman in front of us on her earrings. She looked stunning in a red-orange sundress and the lacy Spanish-style silver earrings studded with tiny rhinestones. "Here take them, they are a gift," she said. No, I protested, she mustn't, but she unhooked them from her ears and placed them right in my hand. When I said I didn't wear big earrings, she had me put them right on. I took her address and later sent her a pair of mine. When I got home, my daughter, who works in the medical field, insisted I wash them in Clorox®, saying I could contract a disease and must never try on earrings at a store.

Historical Importance of Earrings

arrings were first worn as amulets against evil spirits and as good luck charms. In time, they became decorative objects, and eventually, as the most visible piece of jewelry, they signaled wealth and prestige. Earrings became so elaborate and expensive that they presented the ostentation of the rich versus the drabness of poor commoners. Across all social and economic boundaries, the art of jewelry was connected with sexual favors — men using it to bribe women into acceptance and women wearing pieces to attract eligible men as admirers and protectors.

Jewelry was also part of the artistry of humans. Art objects were intended to become valuable gifts or as a reward for something important or very pleasant. The more advanced tribal life was, the more likely it included crafts in wood, bronze, iron, and, later, silver and gold, which included jewelry making.

Inter-tribal trade consisted not only of vital necessities, like animals, food, tools, and cloths, but also decorative objects, among them, earrings. It is amazing that thousands of years before our modern era, earrings were created using almost the identical fishhooks, snap ties, screw backs, and other sophisticated devices to attach an ornament to the ear as are used today. Similarly, the ancient earrings reproduced on a minuscule scale a great variety of animals and birds or simply showed imaginative symbols — just as they do today.

It is unlikely that the Egyptian or Minoan Crete civilization spread across the Mediterranean into savage mainland Europe. Nor is it likely that distant Chinese, Indian, or Assyrian cultures, including the art of making jewelry, had much influence on Europe at that time, but the Bronze Age brought an awareness of gold as a most rare and precious metal, and since 4000 BC, the first European goldsmiths put their talents to good use. In about 2500 BC, a thousand years before King Tut, Queen Poabi of Sumeria wore large gold crescents with her jeweled headdress, excavated at the royal tombs at

Marilyn Monroe.
Source: The Image Works.

Ur. After gold, silver was the chosen metal for making jewelry, followed by easy-to-model bronze.

Exchangeable objects of value were very portable, serving as barter, and could be used to buy large products. Suddenly, a tribe rich in gold objects was subject to attack by poor and unskilled neighbors who coveted their possessions. The gold-rich tribe might try to buy peace, but this only delayed another predatory attack. The defendants often hid their jewelry in containers placed in deep holes in the ground, treasures that thousands of years later we discovered by accident; thus, in many cases, the discovery of an earring helped to rewrite ancient history by shedding light on how humans lived and their level of civilization.

Glass Beads for Earrings

About 1200 AD, Venice revived the art of making glass and became the glass capital of the world. The many visitors to Venice usually arrived by sea. Travelers whose ships arrived at night saw a faint red glow over a section of the city and flaring red glows over the harbor island, Murano. The haloes came from the glass-making shops, called glasshouses, whose furnaces were turned off only for infrequent repairs and holidays. The craftsmen worked twelve-hour shifts through day and night. Each glasshouse had a specialty: plates, vases, eyeglasses, or mirrors, and many, mostly on Murano, made beads.

Beads became the heart of the glass industry. The merchants who traded in China, Sumatra, India, Baghdad, Africa, and, later, the New World required glass beads to exchange for silk, porcelain, spices, ivory, slaves, and beaver pelts. Originally, all the glasshouses were in Venice, but, in 1291, the city's governing council ordered glasshouses with large furnaces to relocate on Murano, purportedly to protect the inhabitants from the fire hazard of the glass furnaces. However, their real motive was to keep the formulas of glass-making secret. Venetian glass was the best in the world because the master glassmakers had, by experiment, learned, first, the correct proportion of silica, salts, lime, and other minerals to make different kinds and colors of glass and, second, how to reheat and cool glass to make it strong. The penalty for revealing these secrets to anybody outside of Venice was death.

Of all the artisans in Venice — stonemasons, goldsmiths and silversmiths, weavers, and tailors — only the glassmakers were given the rank of burgher, or business person, and allowed to marry daughters of the noble families. Such alliances gave the glassmakers high status, although they lived on Murano like carefully watched prisoners. The Committee of Ten, charged by the council to keep watch on the glassmakers, did not question a master glass-maker suspected of selling his secrets. It simply hired an assassin who, in the dead of night, stabbed the glassmaker to death and threw his body into a canal. "He was eaten by the salamander," the residents of Murano would say, believing that a salamander, the animal sacred to the alchemist, lived in every glass-making furnace.

At first, the beadmakers formed one of five glassmakers' guilds. The other four guilds made bottles, mirrors, crystal, and glassware. With the expansion of the bead business, the beadmakers' guild split into two by specialty — small beads or large. Small beads were the ordinary, single-colored beads that traders used as currency. Some large beads also went for trade, but most of them ended up in fancy rosaries, necklaces, and earrings. The guilds controlled wages, terms of apprenticeship, quality of beads, and prices. Of the thousands of Venetian youth that wanted to join the beadmakers' guilds every year, only a few were chosen and these often were the sons of the glassmakers.

Star beads and *millefiori* were the most spectacular designs. Around 1600, 2,515 bead furnaces were making drawn beads from molten glass on Murano, and one hundred beadmakers were making wire-wound beads in smaller furnaces in Venice. Throughout the seventeenth and eighteenth centuries, the industry produced between five hundred and eight hundred pounds of beads a day, or between 175,000 and 280,000 pounds per year. After Napoleon conquered Venice, bead production fell off, but, by 1850, demand for beads to trade with Native Americans in the American West revived the bead industry. Mass production and handmade beads for earrings now come from India, Japan, and Czechoslovakia. Yahhazie, whose work is shown in Chapter 15, is a member of the Shoshone people, and prides herself in using Czech glass beads.

Ancient Trading

At the personal level, making a piece of jewelry had clear mercantile advantages for its creator: he could ask any amount of money on top of the cost of precious metal. The more sophisticated the design of an earring, and the better it looked when hung from the lobe, the more money he could ask. In the last few thousand years, one truth about a piece of jewelry has never changed: if the buyer likes it and wants it, the price can hardly be negotiated.

Any piece of jewelry was universal currency before the appearance of coins. As for the coin, it had to be created out of something that did not rust and it needed to be impossible to duplicate, in order to prevent forgery. The latter was accomplished by having an elaborate design on both faces of the coin: one showing the figure of the ruler who minted the coin, including his name, while the other side showed the value of the coin and a design of something important, like a divinity, temple, or animal. Roman and Greek coins followed this pattern of stamping a coin. When it came to beauty and obvious value, nothing came closer to an art object than a coin—making it the first choice for an earring. An attached clasp, or a simple hole drilled in a side of a coin, made it possible to hang it with string or a hook to the ear lobe. Often it was matched by a pendant using a matching coin.

This essay is the work of Ion Grumeza, a Romanian-born scholar and author of several non-fiction history books, including Dacia: Land of Transylvania, Cornerstone of Ancient East Europe. *Ion lives, writes, and teaches in Louisville, Kentucky.*

Celts, Byzantine, and Medieval

"
And she took sandals upon her feet, and put about her bracelets, and her chains, and her earrings.
"

~ Book of Judith 10:4

Celts and Dacians

by Ion Grumeza, Historian

In Ancient Europe, the most prolific jewelry makers were the Celts, whose core population of some two hundred powerful tribes populated the continent from the Britannica islands to Gaul/Gallic lands and extended into Eastern Europe, into Dacia (ancient Romania) and south of the Lower Danube into the Balkan Peninsula. Tall and strong people who believed in many gods, the Celts proved such fearsome warriors that, in the first century BC, they became a threat to the Roman Republic, which was also in full expansion. The Celts were not only a military might, but also a cultural and religious one, since, due to their advanced metallurgic skills, they had mastered the creation of the best weapons of the time. These skills were greatly applied to the craft of jewelry making, much in demand in Athens and Rome, as well as by rich barbarian tribes. The Gallic torque, or metal collar, was their trademark, and it was the only piece of property the naked warriors carried in battle. Their earrings, based on the same string design, were a natural complement in their expensive appearance. Of course, their coins were easily converted into earrings.

One of their specialties was the Celtic swirl-design earring dating from 500 BC. Most probably, a matching Celtic swirl pendant, having some religious significance, similar to the Celtic endless knot, accompanied these.

The advanced Celtic art of making jewelry, implicitly earrings, used melted, colorful glass that ornamented so many other objects, including swords and shields. The sophistication of the Celtic earring design is in sharp contrast to the simple silver loops of Scandinavian extraction and Roman gold loops of a similar concept and lesser sophistication. In a society where men competed with women in wearing jewelry, the craft was often dominated by masculine taste.

Gaulish bracelet and earrings from the princely tomb of Sainte. Colombe, Cote d'Azur (6th to 5th century BC).
Source: Gaulish, Musee des Antiquites Nationales, St. Germaine-en-Loys, France, Bridgeman Art Library.

Greek cow's head pendants (5th century BC).
Source: The Walters Art Museum.

Crimean woman's heads wearing earrings (4th century BC).
Source: The State Hermitage Museum, St. Petersburg. Vladimir Terebin, Leonard Kheifets, Yuri Molodkovets, photographers.

Boat-shaped with granulation (3rd century BC).
Source: The State Hermitage Museum, St. Petersburg. Vladimir Terebin, Leonard Kheifets, Yuri Molodkovets, photographers.

Eros pendants (3rd century BC).
Source: The State Hermitage Museum, St. Petersburg. Vladimir Terebin, Leonard Kheifets, Yuri Molodkovets, photographers.

Tribal existence on Central European land was shaken by Julius Caesar, who, for eight years (58–50 BC), endeavored to defeat the Gallic tribes and extend the Roman borders to the Rhine River. After one million were killed and two million taken into slavery, the remaining Celts did everything they could to escape the punishing legions. The logical direction for them to head was toward unknown Eastern Europe, where the only consolidated power was that of the Dacians (old Romanians). The Celts mastered the land from what is today Bohemia, to near Odessa (Ukraine), and from Slovakia to the Balkan Mountains. It turned out that the peaceful Celtic invasion in Dacia was most beneficial for all the tribes involved and ensured a long-lasting coexistence. The Celts brought the fine crafts, and the Dacians provided the gold and silver from their famous mines of Transylvania. Because the new settlers introduced revolutionary tools, such as the iron plough, the pottery revolving table, construction tools, and, most of all, advanced weaponry, they helped the Dacians become the third economic and military power of Europe.

The lavish presence of silver and gold allowed the Dacian numerous aristocracy to use precious metals for each accessory of their fashion, from fibulas, buttons, clasps, chains, bracelets, coils, necklaces, and torques (obvious a Celtic influence) to earrings of round shape, thicker in the middle with incrustations. Since Dacians were the wolf worshipers, many ends of their spiral bracelets and earrings represented the beloved wolf head.

Scythian.
Source: Art Resource,
New York.

SCYTHIAN ARTISTRY

Because of gold, rich Dacia was the target for Scythian invasions, which, in part, ended in a peaceful coexistence, actually forming a tribal federation of Getians along the last leg of the Danube River. The Getians' goldsmiths were strongly influenced by Greek and Roman designs from jewelry bought by merchants along the west coast of the Black Sea and the mouth of the Danube. Located between the civilized and barbarian worlds, the Getians could acquire the best from both civilizations' earring craft. Other Scythians spent only years in Dacia, deciding to migrate northeast into today's Ukraine, where their horses could benefit from the vast pastures. Some chieftains buried their gold treasures in Dacia before leaving, and in 1837, twenty-two pieces of gold items weighing nineteen kilograms were discovered at Pietroasa, Romania. Mainly large objects, like flat plates and cups, but also fibulas/broaches and two bracelets with precious stones, have been found, hidden in the ground since a short time after the death of Jesus. All show a masterful hand in the making of such artistic objects.

Because Scythian men wore earrings, one can imagine the demand for such ornamental objects shaped in a "U" form with birds, snakes, and animals at the end of the lever back. The mounted warriors prized their earrings and rings on each finger, indicating the clan, the tribe, the rank, and other distinctive functions in society. The blond, blue-eyed Scythians were excellent warriors who believed gold and blood were powerfully connected to the sun and afterlife. Their military uniforms were colored in yellow and red, and highly decorated with gold motifs. They wore a large gold earring in the left ear. Women were equal to men, and probably wore earrings in each ear, matching the one that the men wore.

Their horse culture seemed not to interfere with their art of making jewelry. It is not clear what kind of heritage produced such advanced jewelry makers, but in the port of Olbia (near today's Odessa) of their kingdom, the Scythians traded with established Greek colonies. They exchanged their jewelry for Greek products, mostly ceramic containers, which happened to be filled with wine. So, when a great pair of earrings is found in the Hellenistic world, most likely it is not Greek-made.

The Scythians sent their dead to the afterlife with adornment. For example, a fourth-century pair of earrings from a woman's grave, discovered in a burial mound in the Ukraine and now in the Ukrainian Museum of Historical Treasures in Kiev, have not only filigree and granulation, but a skein of ducks. Ducks cap the finials of the two ends of each hollow boat shape, from which duck-shaped pendants hang. By stamping and assembling hollow parts, the Scythian goldsmith made big earrings more wearable. He also aimed for the earrings to "clack" attractively as a woman turned her head.

Other mega-invaders were the Sarmatian tribes with a similar culture and interest in jewelry. The horsemen and their women, many of them also warriors, wore spiral earrings and expensive jewelry. The goldsmiths mastered the gold-leafing of bronze earrings and added beautiful beads to their creations. They seem to have had their own gold supply, but nothing compared to the mines of Dacia. For the sake of gold, many invading tribes accepted the suzerainty of the Dacians and became loyal settlers — except the Iazygi, the early greedy Sarmatians who kept waging war because they always wanted the best mines with precious metals. However, the Dacian gold and silver nuggets could buy-out any barbarian leader with bellicose ideas.

The ten-gram *coson* was the Dacian currency made of 22-karat gold, standing out even today among the purest coins ever minted. *Cosons* played a role in the Roman civil war after the murder of Caesar in 44 BC. His assassin, Marcus Brutus, fled into Roman-occupied Balkans and used the Dacian coins to pay his loyal legions.

Emerald pendants
(6th century AD).
Source: The Walters
Art Museum.

Basket style (7th
century AD). Source:
The Walters Art Museum.

PAX ROMANA...AND EXTRAVAGANCE

The Roman takeover of Transylvania, rich in gold beyond description, was the only invasion to have a long-lasting impact on the Dacians. In 106 A.D., Emperor Trajanus crowned his victory with the title "Dacicus Maximus" and brought from Dacia to Rome 165 tons of gold and 364 tons of silver. Trajan's Column, erected one hundred feet high in the middle of the Forum with the same name, was built in the center of Rome with Dacian gold and Dacian slave labor. Many of the column's friezes show the plunder of Transylvania. Among the Dacian prisoners are sculpted numerous women holding their babies: the women have sophisticated hairdos with diadems and many appear to wear earrings, probably *cosoni* — an expected accessory to match and complete their dignified appearance.

Because of the partial conquest of Dacia, the Roman Empire prospered for the next one hundred years, and Roman peace never looked better in history. With it came an unprecedented era of luxury reflected in extravagant jewelry — a true Golden Age of Roman society. Roman earrings were made of gold loops with colorful glass beads and pendants. Gold studs were also common. Aristocratic women displayed their wealth by wearing earrings with emeralds, rubies, sapphires, and topaz, which matched their finger rings and necklaces, sometimes accompanied by sparkling tiaras. It's well known that Lollia Paulina, Emperor Caligula's wife, loved emeralds and pearls and jewelry that included earrings. Eventually, Rome's thirst for a luxurious life and the eroding power of the legions spread all over the world and led to the unavoidable: the empire collapsed from within and became prey for new waves of barbarians, from Huns to Goths. The ancient world of Europe was over, mainly because the Roman emperors ran out of gold to pay its legions and bribe the attacking barbarians.

Byzantine Drops and Crosses

The Middle Ages began in Eastern Europe with countless invaders coming from Eurasia, all leading their horses to Rome and Byzantium, renamed Constantinople, the most fortified and richest city in the Balkans. In order to prove their Roman roots, the Byzantines donned gold jewelry, distinctively oversized and ornamented with colorful stones. Their earrings followed the same heavy pattern, often designed as a cross in tribute to Christian devotion. Orthodoxy preached against, or did not encourage, the use of precious embellishments, like earrings, unless the believer was an aristocrat.

Such types of heavy jewelry matched the expensive colorful silk attire with gold thread and colorful stones worked into the fabric. The ascetic icon-like paintings of the time show emperors and empresses, aristocrats and other powerful individuals portrayed in a flat dimension, with saintly faces, but lavish clothes and impressive amounts of gold ornaments. Even Jesus, who is typically modestly dressed, holds a Bible with thick covers, studded with gold, precious stones, and expensive designs. One of the first emperors, Justinian I, was a son of a peasant, but judging by his portrait done in mosaic, he very soon learned the powerful importance of dazzling jewels, including a colorful golden crown and a round mantle clasp rimmed with white pearls — he wears four pearl drop earrings.

Byzantine earrings were designed to attract immediate attention by having emeralds, garnets, pearls, rubies, and other precious stones hanging by gold chains from ear loops. To show humility and total faith in the Church, a beautiful gold cross prominently hung at the base of the earrings.

For the rest of medieval history, until the fall of Constantinople in 1453, the emperors competed in military glory, donning magnificent rich costumes and jewelry to match. Fathers killed or blinded their sons who aspired to the throne, brothers butchered brothers, and empresses assassinated their husbands — all while sporting expensive and lavish earrings, particularly pearls.

WARS OVER JEWELRY

In fact, and possibly uniquely in history, one of the most unforeseen invasions and sieges of Constantinople was carried out by Sultan Bayezid I, who was extremely envious of the bejeweled Byzantine society. Shortly after 1390, the Byzantine clergy invited Bayezid to hunt in their land. They hoped to obtain his benevolence, but instead the outraged sultan saw firsthand how rich the empire was. A dashing dresser who wore an earring with a dropped pearl, the sultan was so eaten up by greed that he led an army to conquer what he saw: people covered with elaborate jewelry.

The Turkish invasion, led by Sultan Mehmed II, marked the unstoppable rise of the Ottoman Empire, which eventually would occupy Constantinople and the entire Balkan Peninsula. The pillage of Ottoman soldiers looking for gold and jewelry reached apocalyptic proportions and not even the sacred Hagia Sofia was spared. The divine icons of the magnificent cathedral were smashed and stripped of gold and silver by the victors, their horses waiting nearby to carry away the precious loot.

Byzantine chain link pendants (7th century AD). Source: The Walters Art Museum.

One century later, the Ottoman Court hired almost one hundred jewelry designers to please the royal members and fill the demands of the harem that numbered a few hundred beauties from all over the world. Emerald and rubies seemed to be the favorite precious stones, while gold and ivory were abundantly featured as decorations on clothing and personal objects. Jewels were also heavily used to adorn weapons. Head-plumes of egret feathers enhanced the fashion for women and soon were adopted by men; and then even clipped to the horses' heads. Imaginative floral designs of these *aigrettes* increased the dazzling reflections of diamonds and other precious gems.

The earrings were dropped pearls with two or three strings. The longer the strings, the more impressive and expensive the earrings. The elite competed in the length of the dangling earrings. The wife of Sultan Mustafa II was known for her pearls, with diamond and emerald strings that hung to her knees. Common women used dangling coins, which also proved to make lovely necklaces of many rows around the neck; soon they began using the necklaces to frame the forehead and then their entire head. Eventually, the string of coins served as a belt around the waist or bracelets for hands and feet. Since coins glittered in the sunshine, made appealing noises, and advertised the wealth of the bride-to-be, soon the entire Balkan population was copying the fashion. A popular earring design was in the shape of a crescent and many creative versions underlined faith in Allah.

DIFFERENT KINDS OF EARRINGS

A Gothic style of earrings featured the predictable designs of bats, dragons, snakes, skulls, spiders, and spikes, not necessarily dangling on loops, but often attached to different parts of the ears. The pieces were mainly made of pewter and reflected the beliefs in superstition and protective talismans. They were connected to the revolutionary church architecture, and a further statement of the new protestant movement.

Crowns with Earrings to Match

(Russia and East Europe)

The most expensive jewelry in the Middle Ages was the crown for emperors, czars, princes, warlords, and other rulers, yet the most dazzling were often the crowns and tiaras of their wives. In modern day, Eastern Europe and Russia have astonishing examples of necklaces and earrings coordinated with the royal crowns. Diamonds of different colors seemed to be the preferred stone. A painting of Catherine the Great shows the imperial crown topped with a diamond cross next to her while she holds a commanding yet delicate scepter and displays earrings that are shaped like a fan and use multiple dropped strings of diamonds (a design now called chandelier). These were obviously influenced by Byzantine culture. A matching double string choker with thousands of diamonds completes her majestic image.

Russian nobility tried their best to imitate the monarch, and the rest of Eastern Europe aimed to copy their taste in jewelry. The commoners went for practical, less expensive materials, using copper, amber, and beads. Natural flowers were a material within reach: beautiful plants could be shaped as tiaras, and "earrings" moved to the top of the ear in the form of a colorful blooming flower. Adorned thus with flowers, a woman had no need of mascara — a very important cosmetic treatment at this time. Ultimately, the goldsmith or other jewelry makers would copy these motifs for their work. While Russian women still prefer precious jewelry, as has been their tradition for centuries, Polish and other Eastern European women, who traditionally did not have the money for elaborate jewels, tend to treasure any inexpensive artifact.

Lombard
multicolored cross
motif with stone
or glass inlays
(7th century AD).
Source: The Walters Art
Museum.

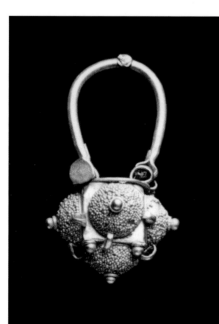

Granulated gold
(10th century AD).
Source: The Walters
Art Museum.

Celtic from Spain.
Source: Archaeological
Museum of Spain, Art
Resource, New York.

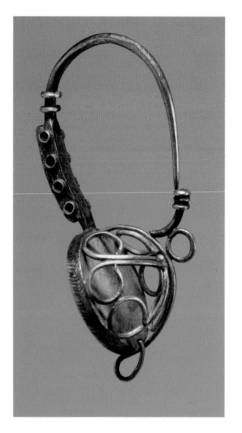

Medieval gold loops.
Source: The Walters Art Museum.

SALBA OF ROMANIA

Women of Romania, where I grew up, tend to wear their jewelry proudly and frequently. Traditionally, a Romanian woman advertises her wealth with *salba,* or gold coin necklaces, smartly arranged by the size of the coins, with the smaller ones, *cocoseii* or *mahmudele,* in the back and the larger coins, *galben* or *napoleon,* as the center piece, resting between the breasts. *Cocoseii,* the name for small Ottoman coins, refers to little coins depicting a rooster. *Galben* is the mispronounced Dutch *gulden,* the great large coin usually from the Frantz Joseph reign. *Napoleon* is the mythical name for the most expensive gold coin on the market; it has a diameter of almost one inch. Single or multiple strings of *salba* of different lengths can cover the entire chest area with glittering gold pieces. Naturally, earrings of dangling gold coins match the impressive display of a portable mini-treasury. This custom is so old and well-rooted in the Romanian culture that even when the Communist regime took by force all the gold from the citizens, *salba* and earrings were immune from confiscation, as they were considered to be an endowment from parents and grandparents.

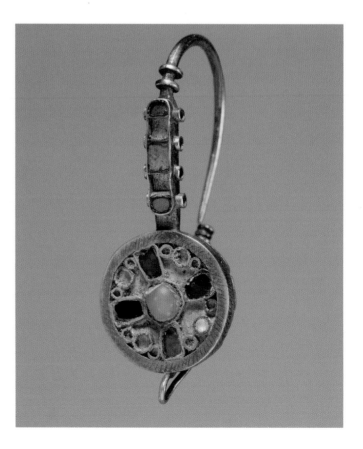

Basket style
(6th century AD).
Source: Walters Art Museum.

ROMANY

Romany, or Gypsy, men have traditionally worn earrings in the shape of hoops of different sizes. Gypsy women are known even more for their love of jewelry. Migratory people from Baluchistan into the earlier Ottoman Empire, the Romany proved their skill as horse-breeders, master ironworkers, and jewelry makers. Over the ages, often banned and expelled, they wore their valuables: for women that was gems, silver and old gold coins, adornments on ears and hair, as well as scarves and clothing.

Highly needed in the Turkish army to shoe horses and fix firearms, the Romany sold jewelry as peddlers throughout the Balkans. Prince Vlad III, Dracula of the Romanian principality, brought them north of the Danube in 1461 into the heart of Europe, hoping to put their age-old skills to use by teaching their craftsmanship to Romanians. The Romany migrated to all cardinal points, peddling their silver and gold trade, with the women making money as fortune-tellers. Highly artistic people in singing, playing instruments, and dancing, their earrings reflect their mysterious identity.

Earrings … Gifts to be Passed Down

As the Middle Ages progressed, each nation and country shaped the image of its own style of jewelry, and since they seem to be the permanent fixture in any woman's attire, earrings remained the most versatile pieces. They were the first gift presented to a girl after she pierced her ears, and the relatively inexpensive cost allowed even a poor person to own more than one pair.

Regardless of the time period, geographic region, and cultural heritage, earrings can be seen to have crossed all borders, making a universal statement of beautifully crafted adornments. They often remain in families, passed down from generation to generation. In addition to their financial value, earrings often have sentimental value, making them neither appraisable nor transferable. Easy to hide in case of danger, they have proven through the ages to be a possession one can carry anyplace.

A pair of earrings tells a lot about the personality of their owner. Additionally, their power to impress and to make a larger cultural statement remains timeless, just like a military uniform or a piece of fine furniture. In many cases, earrings are the first things to be noticed about a woman. This fact alone speaks for their importance. Certainly earrings are precious heirlooms throughout the millenniums, for they magically carry family and cultural heritages.

Renaissance Europe

> *FULVIA:* Bring my Glass and Table hither.
> *GALLA:* Madam.
> *FULVIA:* Look Within, i' my blue Cabinet,
>   for the Pearl I had sent me last,
>   and bring it.
> *GALLIA:* That from Clodius?
> *FULVIA:* From Caius Caesar.
>   You are for Clodius still.
> *GALLIA:* Is this it, Madam?
> *FULVIA:* Yes, help to hang it in my Ear.
> *GALLIA:* Believe me,
>   It is a rich one, Madam.
> *FULVIA:* I hope so: It should not be
>   worn there else.
>
> ~ Ben Jonson, *Catiline His Conspiracy (1611)*

A Dainty Comeback

Jewelry we see from this period, in museum cases and portraits, looks like costume from a fairy tale or Shakespeare production — and it was, for the theater of royal life. It tended towards gorgeousness, with colorful stones, elaborately set singularly or massed in clusters, creating the ooh-ah effect. Silver was used in some earrings to make the metal setting less visible. No longer needed for ecclesiastical symbolism, jewelry exhibited material wealth and symbolized beauty in the here and now. It was in a class with clothing, household furniture, and other moveable goods that a woman could inherit. This gave weight to owning and displaying it: "This is mine."

ISABELLA OF CASTILLE

After a long hiatus from royal courts and aristocratic circles, earrings began their comeback in Spain, awash in gold from the New World. Spanish royalty were clearly eager to show their wealth on their persons. Queen Isabella (1474-1504) donated her golden jewelry to launch Columbus's expedition. She had loads to spare, though we can't see beneath her pious headdress. The Pope declared her and Ferdinand "the Catholic monarchs" for their role in "purifying the faith" by expelling Jews and Muslims from Spain, and earrings would have been too frivolous for her religious leadership.

However, as the century progressed, in southern Europe first, earrings became elaborate *tours de force*. In the 1530s, women's dress style began to ask for adornment around the face, and earrings showed up on portraits and effigies and in the inventories of personal royal belongings. The style was to part the hair, draw it back, and put a pendant in your ear. Combining ribbons, filigree, rose diamonds, and big stones in gold and silver scrollwork and foliage, earrings enlivened a noblewoman's dress, accentuating the major bling. Spanish women wore pairs of teeny carved rock crystal ships as well as

Anne Boleyn (c. 1520-36).
Source: RMN-Grand Palais, Art Resource, New York.

drop pearls. Hoops encircled dogs, eagles, dolphins, sea horses, and rabbits. Some earrings, called *poma* (fruit), were filled with fragrance.

The low bodices fashionable in Europe favored jewelry as well. A woman of high-ranking might wear a pearl drop on a link or several pearls from a gold piece set with a gem. She would not be content with the simple hoop that many women and children (and a few men) had been wearing all along. By 1500, printing presses all over Europe spread technical knowledge among jewelers and goldsmiths; they purchased and used design books illustrated with copper plate etchings. This gave their work a certain unity of style. Renaissance goldsmiths made fabulous pendants with the motifs of mythical heroes and beasts, surrounded by enamel and gold and inlaid with gems and big yellow, pink, or white irregular pearls — the most prized objects of adornment.

Two paintings by Paolo Veronese (1528-88) frame the door to one of the grand galleries at the Frick Museum in New York City. To the left, *Choice of Hercules* shows the Greek hero, dressed in contemporary Venetian garb, choosing lady Virtue over lady Vice. As he ascends to lady Virtue, standing tall, Hercules looks back at lady Vice, crouching below. She holds a book and wears a pearl drop earring. A dark bare-breasted woman crouches beneath her. This shade indicates that the wages of vice are death. In the other painting, *Wisdom and Strength*, lady Wisdom stands tall and dominant over mister Strength, who slouches. Lady Wisdom wears a pearl drop earring, even though she disdains a crown and royal jewels scattered on the ground.

In the two paintings, earrings grace the ears of women of opposite character. In the first, the pearl is ephemeral and will dissolve in the waywardness of sin. In the second, lady Wisdom looks heavenward toward eternal light — a light the earring reflects. As long as there is wisdom, the earring will last. The two paintings indicate that the pearl earring lacked a fixed symbolic value. It was a popular jewel that refracts different light in many stories.

In the Uffizi Gallery, in Florence, a tapestry called *Festa sulla acqua et assalto a un isola* portrays husband and wife leaning towards each other, both with hair pulled off the face, wearing similarly gorgeous dress, with high collars (his, the circus dog style; hers, the standing kind). His head ornament, a kind of pheasant feather embedded with a central jewel, must have had the briefest fashion while she has pearls arranged on her forehead, suspended from a lacy cap. They are sumptuously elegant and aristocratic to the last note of the pendant earring each wears. He is to her left and his earring is on his left ear; verso for her, where she has the pearl on her right ear. We want to peek around each noble head to see whether there is a second earring, but visually striking is that they are one plus one. Formally framed by the earrings, the couple are an inseparable, harmonic pair.

MANNERIST PROPS

In the late 1500s, Mannerist painters favored an ideal of feminine beauty that included extended limbs, long necks, and a slender, sinuous body. This model of perfection spread from Florence to France, and goldsmiths, most notably Benvenuto Cellini, went to Fontainebleau at the invitation of Francois I.

According to art historian Kenneth Clark, "The goddess of mannerism is the eternal feminine of the fashion plate." This mannerist ideal's jewelry were pendants that dripped from the ears; not only girandoles (chandeliers), but also the drop-by-drop pendants called *pendeloques*. The Mannerists liked bare skin and dark backgrounds, which were ideal for using light spots at the ears. A famous Mannerist painting (by Parmigianino), now in Naples, shows a girl, Antea, elongated, with piercing dark eyes, and wearing rich, embroidered clothing and a marten's fur stole; just the two bright lights of the earrings accent the pure oval of her face.

Late Renaissance Period

ELEANORA

Until near extinction of royal houses after World War I, royalty usually married royalty. In the 1500s, kings and queens shipped their daughters to courts to solidify international alliances. The Spanish monarchs, Ferdinand and Isabella, sent Catherine to England to wed Arthur, heir apparent. When Arthur died, Catherine stayed in England with her enormous dowry and married Arthur's brother, Henry. Catherine, though, was not Henry's first marital interest. The initial object of his ambition was Eleanora of Austria (1498–1558) who would have brought to England an extravagant collection of earrings. However, Henry favored an alliance with powerful Spain over the Austrian princess and instead wed Catherine, Eleanora's aunt.

Eleanora was a teenager when her older brother, Charles V, heard whispers of an affair, and found a love letter to her from Frederick II Palatine. Charles expelled Frederick from the court and sent Eleanora off to Portugal to marry King Manual, by whom she bore two children. Manual died of the plague and, in 1530, Eleanora was packed off to France to marry Francois I, with "stones as big as nuts in her ears." Francois, forced by international politics into this marriage, was displeased and he greeted the new queen by appearing with his mistress at a window for all to see.

Eleanora of Austria is a poster girl for the Late Renaissance because she was a sophisticate who lived in three countries (Austria, Spain, and France) and her gigantic, double pear drops gave her some of the self-assurance she surely needed to thrive in the royal match-making game. In a Joos van Cleve portrait, she looks out, pensive and forbearing, from inside a cage of garlands on her head, neck, and across her body. Her earring is both extravagant and integrated into the proliferation of her other pendants. On the side of her head, a huge jewel is tied into her coiffeur. A drop pendant

Giuseppe Arcimboldo, *Archduchess Anna of Austria,* Queen of Spain.
Source: Erich Lessing Art Resource.

pins her necklace into two loops of beads at her chest and, despite the coil of hair that covers her ear, we see a large elliptical gold hoop from which hang three sizable pearl drops.

Fashion merged with symbolism to make pearls the queen of earrings in the 1500s. Until the mid-1500s, people accepted, from the Roman Pliny, that when a shellfish opened a dewdrop entered and transformed into a pearl. The quality of the pearl depended on the purity of the dewdrop. Pearls were thought to have healing properties. Because of their association with the moon, pearls also suggested female fertility and pregnancy. The pearl that drops decorates the clothing, ears,

Joos van Cleve, *Eleanore of Austria* (1530).
Source: Kunst Historisches Museum, Vienna.

and hair of Marcus Gheeraert the Younger's paintings of pregnant women at the English Tudor court.

Paintings of earrings went through a tripartite transformation in sixteenth-century portraits. First of all, the development of oil paint meant the artist could show the optical effects of light on jewelry. Gheeraert, for instance, was an early painter who used a canvas in England. Secondly, depicting a woman in her earrings symbolized that artfulness was superior to the natural. Thirdly, the goddesses often wear earrings, sometimes little else, suggesting that a woman is worthy to be a goddess and could possess *grazia divina*.

DIANE DE POITIERS

Henri II of France was a bold man who wore a trim beard, rakish hat, and a pendant earring — a diamond cut in the shape of a pyramid reflecting light on the polished surfaces. His mistress, Diane de Poitier (1499–1566), was Europe's first famous royal courtesan and an emblem of ageless beauty. She became his lover after widowhood when she was thirty-two and he was twelve. The fact that, for a time, he shared her with his father, Francois I, may be calumny leveled by her enemies. For this early period, signature images are the paintings by miniaturist and portraitist Francois Clouet. In a 1571 painting at the National Gallery in Washington, D.C., Diane sits naked to the waist and wears a coronet of seed pearls on her crown of braids, one drop pearl hanging over her high forehead, and drop-shaped pearl earrings framing her oval face. In spite of the jewelry, it is the native beauty and insouciance that impress us.

According to Flaubert, the spectacular castle that Henri had constructed for Diane over the Cher River was "built on the water and into the air." Henri gave Diane many of the crown jewels, which, under royal rules, was the primary way a woman could have something to keep as a life insurance policy on the king. Henri gave her the legendary Briolette (Pear) of India; at ninety carats and flawless, it is one of the most famous diamonds in the world, which Diane could wear as a pendant or earring (presumably tied to her hair due to its weight). Elinor of Aquitaine had brought this gem to England in the twelfth century, and her son, Richard the Lionhearted, took it on crusade. It next appeared when Henri gave it to Diane. The Briolette then disappeared until 1950, when Harry Winston bought it from an Indian maharaja.

Diane was slender, with strong shoulders, small hands, high breasts, and alabaster skin. Henri's queen, Catherine de Medici, was bright, plump, and homely. Catherine, wearing her best dress in an enamel (1555) by Leonard Limosin, has dark, gray pearls everywhere on her clothes, hair, and ears. Contrastingly, Diane favored the somber elegance of black and white, particularly black satin, and very décolletage. As lovers, Henri and Diane were discreet, but at his coronation it was obvious Diane had the king's heart, for Henri wore, in the fleur-de-lys of his brocade smock, the monogram "H.D." interlaced.

Although twenty years older than the king, Diane followed a regimen of riding and swimming in the Cher and drank a gold elixir. She became a myth of Diane/Venus in her own time. Pierre Ronsard and Joachim du Bellay raved in their poetry that she outshone the sun and the moon. Portraits of Diane *à la toilette,* or "in her bath," abound. She may be shown naked to her navel, dressed in merely a filmy see-through cape and earrings, but, with the posture of a dancer, she always has an *allure imposante* and looks demure. Of all the legendary women in this book, I think Diane glows with the most pearlescent beauty, utterly at one with her pearl drops.

When Henri II died in a joust in 1559, Catherine evicted Diane from her castle Chenonceaux and took back the crown jewels. Diane's tomb was destroyed during the French Revolution; her body was exhumed and her bones were taken to the town churchyard. Sources claimed that the gold content of her body was 250 times higher than normal. Through her second daughter, Anne, duchesse d'Aumale, were descended thirteen kings and a queen: four kings of France, four kings and a queen of Spain, four kings of Sardinia, and one king of Sicily. She was overheard saying to Henri that she was worthy to bear his royal children and history vindicated her amply on this point.

VERONICA FRANCO

The most famous of the many glamorous courtesans of sixteenth century Venice was Veronica Franco (1546–1591). At the time, high-class courtesans lived in luxurious apartments, dressed with elegance, and cultivated refinements like poetry and music. They moved in humanistic circles, like the *salonistes* later in France, where women dressed to the hilt, sharpened their wits and skills at playing musical instruments and recitation, and could be both seen and heard. Courtesans were registered legally and paid high taxes to the Serenissimo or city manager. Travel guides advertised courtesans as tourist attractions. Montaigne made an extensive visit to Venice and described the courtesans as bejeweled princesses. He also remarked on how businesslike they were about plying their trade.

Veronica learned her trade as the daughter of a courtesan who educated her to be witty and literary, as well as sensuously accomplished. Franco published her own poetry and anthologies of other poets. With her earnings as a courtesan and an author, she supported a household of servants, children, and tutors, and founded a charity for needy courtesans and their children.

Reformist friars railed against Venice's sex trade and managed to bring Franco to trial on charges of magical incantations in her home and as a witch responsible for the plague that snatched the lives of many Venetians. Her long-time friend and perhaps lover defended her and she was acquitted.

The goldsmiths who made Veronica's earrings had workshops on the bridges of Venice because these were the most trafficked and policed places in the city. In portraits, we see Veronica wearing different pairs. In a painting by Tintoretto, Veronica's earrings resemble none other in paintings before or since. Several-tiered, they appear to have bows with a central ruby at the top and then three pearl pendants. The earrings look costly and exotic, feminine and bold. Since Venice had elaborate sumptuary rules for men but not women, the

Tintoretto, *The Meeting of Tamar
and Juda* (1555–1559).
Source: Museo Thyssen- Bornemisza, Madrid.

women could dress in clothes and jewels that communicated the status of their husbands and their individuality. If they strayed too far, a husband or lover could pay the fine!

Veronica wrote Tintoretto that the portrait achieved such likeness that she could have hallucinated it. Unmistakably, Veronica revels in her over-the-top choice of adornment. The earrings also prominently embody the style of girandoles, which would become popular for the next two hundred years. Perhaps Franco even influenced women to wear them, as it was said that Venetian proper women envied the prostitutes' freedom to read what they pleased and mix socially with men.

In a crazy chess move of Renaissance politics, Henri de Valois became king of Poland for less than a year in

1574. When his brother died, he returned to France to become the last Valois king, Henri III, before the Bourbons ascended to France. En route, he passed through Venice. Henri, handsome and literary, looking for a good time and having heard of the courtesans, put the Venetians on their toes. The city fathers especially wanted to make an impression on him because they needed France as an ally against the Turks. The city of Venice treated Henri to ten days of pageantry, during which he spent a night alone with Franco. Later, she addressed letters to the king, in which she figured as Danae and he as Zeus, the same mythological subject Titian used for some of his most famous works. She limns Henri as a "ray of divine virtue" who melted her "natural vigor." On the other hand, he was gossiped about as effeminate — one alternate explanation for a painter's having him share a pair of pearl drops with a noblewoman.

Franco wrote in *terza rima* like Dante, which was tart and rapid and in which she expressed her lively, independent spirit. In her poetry, Veronica simultaneously titillated and criticized the man's world in which she lived. You'll find no broken hearts in her poetry and letters. Rather she fashioned images of the courtesan-poet giving all for love or seeking revenge, or the demanding mistress giving lessons on sexual positions:

> *So sweet and delicious do I become when I find
> myself in bed with a person of whom I feel myself
> loved and enjoyed that the pleasure I bring ex-
> ceeds all delight so that however tight it appeared
> the knot of divine love is tighter still.*

She wrote flattering verse to the city fathers, but she also defended other courtesans "being prey to many men and disease…rushing toward the shipwreck of your mind and body," and called for gender equality: *When we are armed and practiced well, we women/ Can answer for ourselves as well as men can./ Have we not hands and feet and arms like you?* (Terza Rima 16)

England

Across the English Channel, earrings leave the perimeter of Dutch homes and painters' studios for public places. During this period, aristocratic life was organized around the court. Dancing was a crucial accomplishment. In the previous century, the Tudor King, Henry VIII, did a leaping dance called the galliard, which imitated the chase after a woman. His second wife, Anne Boleyn, danced in private, while her daughter, Elizabeth, danced in public, as daily exercise and display of power, everyday for forty years. The new dynasty, the Stuarts, who came to power in 1603, raised the stakes. When James I married Anne of Denmark, the new queen became a royal champion of masques, elaborate dances that combined poetry, costume, and scenery. (The court dress was intermingled with the most fantastical garb and effects.)

A masque was grander than a ball because of its transformative dimension. Anne developed high court culture and traditional Christmas revelries. She was the center of the Stuart court and played all the roles of queen while her courtiers, like flowers in the formal palace garden, did the patterns and steps that cohered them as a court. If you weren't a good dancer, you didn't step out onto the dance floor. James, who was from Scotland and didn't grow up dancing like the London aristocrats, only danced once, tipsy and amorous, abroad in the Jutland peninsula when wooing Anne, but he liked to watch the masques she produced.

Anne's royal marriage had a rough start because the ship she boarded from Denmark to marry James turned back due to stormy seas. Some of the English populace suspected witches at work. Nevertheless, once landed, Anne threw herself into designing fabulous masques. A play, *The Masque of Blackness,* for the second Stuart Christmas (1605), had the theme of pearls. In an opening scene, the women appeared black as the Daughters of Niger accented all the pearls. All the masquers

Margaret Laton (circa 1620).
Source: V&A Images, London, Art Resource, New York.

Robert Peake, *Elizabeth Poulett* (1616).
Source: Photo © Agnew's, London, Bridgeman Art Library.

John de Critz, *Anne of Denmark* (1606-1615).
Source: The Colonial Williamsburg Foundation.
Museum Purchase.

Another contemporary, John Chamberlain, wrote to friends:

> *Whatsoever the device may be and what success they may have in their dancing, yet you would have been sure to have seen great riches in jewels, when one lady, and that under a baroness, is said to be furnished for better than a hundred thousand pounds. And the Lady Arabella goes beyond her; and the queen must not come behind.*

Anne had abundant and exquisite jewelry. She wears different pairs of earrings in her portraits and it would have been a sight to look in her collection. She had round and pear pearls, sometimes combined with diamonds, and diamonds mounted in small, chain loops mixed with opals and rubies, all quite versatile to

entered on a giant concave shell, so they became pearls too. The dresses were azure (like the sea, the source of pearls) and silver, with feathers and jewels; the necklaces, ropes of pearls and diamonds. Contemporary Ben Johnson, in the introduction to the *Masque of Blackness*, wrote: "And for the front, ear, neck, and wrists, the ornament was of the most choice and ornate pearl; best setting off from the black." During the rule of James and Anne, Shakespeare put masques into *Love's Labor's Lost* and other comedies.

Adrian Vanson,
Anne of Denmark
(1595).
Source: Bridgeman
Art Library,
Philip Mould
Ltd.,photographer.

Stuart crystal with Charles I monogram
with plaited hair beneath crystal.
Source: The Three Graces.

transform into some other kind of pendant. From her
favorite jeweler, George Heriot, a Scot, Anne purchased
the lavish baubles she and the dancers required. According to jewelry historian, Diana Scarisbrick (*Jewelry
in Britain, 1066–1837*), the queen also acquired from
Heriot earrings with figurative and naturalistic designs
— diamond African heads, lizards, hands holding snakes,
and a snake with a diamond head.

Critics said Anne bankrupted the kingdom with
the extravagance of her masques, clothes, and building
projects. She had to sell back some jewels to Heriot and
pawned others. However, not only are England's buildings in the Palladian style thanks to her sponsorship of
Inigo Jones, but Shakespeare also received a great boost
when James came to the throne. He flattered James's
Scottish background with *Macbeth* and went on to perform more often before James and Anne than he had for
Elizabeth.

Over the course of the 1600s, the English overthrew
two Stuart kings — once by beheading and once by exile.
Anne's masques may have strained the royal treasury,
but her husband, James I, faced no serious challenges
to his rule. The same was not true for his son and heir,
Charles I. By the time Charles came to the throne in
1625, the English had embraced the Protestant revolution started by Henry VIII in the 1540s. The king had
replaced the pope in English minds and hearts as head
of the church, and Charles alienated pious Anglicans by
marrying Henrietta Maria, a French (and Roman Catholic) princess. He suppressed the more radical Anglicans
who wanted to govern their local churches. Many fled to
America, where we know them as Puritans. Most importantly, Charles ran afoul of Parliament, which refused
to fund the king's ill-fated wars on the Continent. The
struggle between Parliament and the king escalated into
a civil war in which parliamentary forces, led by Oliver
Cromwell, defeated the king, after which Parliament
voted to execute Charles for treason. After a decade of
increasingly dictatorial rule by Oliver Cromwell, Par-

Stuart crystal with gold and silver
Source: Amanda Grove Holmen.

liament reinstated the Stuarts, who remained on the
throne, though with much reduced power, until James
II responded to parliamentary opposition by fleeing to
France.

Charles I went to his execution wearing an earring.
Sometime after the death of Charles, women with royalist sympathies began to wear earrings of faceted rock
crystal holding the king's image or monogram or even a
lock of hair. After the restoration of the Stuarts in 1660,
these "Stuart crystals" became more popular, and after
James II, the last Stuart, fled the country, rock crystal
earrings remained a stylish way to memorialize a figure
of the past or a departed loved one.

Georges de La Tour, *The Cheat* [detail] (1635–40). Source: Erich Lessing, Art Resource, New York.

Charles Beaubrun, *Portrait of a Lady Wearing a Yellow Silk Dress* (1646). Source: Photo © Rafael Valls Gallery, London, Bridgeman Art Library.

France

As the 1600s unfold, the center of haute jewelry moved from Florence to Paris. In 1533, Catherine de Medici put back in their boxes the ruffs brought to France from Italy on her marriage to Henri II, replacing them by swishy very full gowns with padded hips and décolletage. Now the fashionable gathered in elegant furnished rooms rather than big empty halls.

The French noblewoman of the early 1600s might wear a pearl pendant or, as Maria Theresa, queen of Louis XIII, did, two pearls or two pierced pendants. As the century went on, the styles became more opulent. Great quantities of rubies, sapphires, and emeralds, as well as pearls and semi-precious colored stones, such as topazes, turquoise, and coral came from Persia, India, and Ceylon. Diamonds from Indian mines were cut, polished, and faceted in Antwerp, Amsterdam, and Paris. The French royal family initially kept the jewelers busy, as they catered to the demands of Marie de Medici and Henry IV, and later Louis XIV and Madame de Maintenon, that least ostentatious of jewelry buffs, who nevertheless advised the Duchess of Burgundy "to wear jewels so as to draw attention to the clearness of your skin and the neatness of your figure." That the objective was to sparkle and express movement is in the word for the necklace of a stream of graduated stones, the *rivière*.

French schoolchildren and lyceans learn the rule of threes, *la règle des tiers*. The model of the structure in three parts was from ancient Rome — *omne trium perfectum*, as in Caesar's "I saw, I came, I conquered." The grid formed by two horizontal lines and two vertical, known as the Golden Grid, gave an artist a basis for design, where elements were placed on the lines and not dead center; and the playwrights Moliere, Corneille, and Racine capitalized on three actors appearing on stage at once. In my school days, each argument in an essay, or *devoir*, had three parts, so copybooks had folds to accommodate a properly formatted answer. Thus, for earrings it was *de rigueur* in the seventeenth century to have three elements. Typically, there was a hoop, the central

"Mancini pearls" given by Louis XIV to
Marie Mancini (c. mid-17th century).
Source: Private Collection, Christie's Images,
Bridgeman Art Library.

Spain

In the 1600s, Spain was awash in gold from the New World. After a thousand years, during which little gold was mined in Europe, gold was plentiful. The fairy tale writer Countess d'Aulnoy tried to poison her dreadful husband in the Tuileries and was secreted out of jail by her lover, traveling pregnant to Spain on bumpy roads. She wrote a best-selling travelogue, *Voyage d'Espagne* (1690), in which she describes the Spanish court's "taste for earrings as long as a hand and even longer." (Changling animals in her fables wear oversize earrings, too). The heavy earrings required an extra circle of metal soldered on to tie to a lock of hair. They either had satin or velvet bows at the centerpiece or the design where pendant jewels or pearls hung from the central portion, thus the girandole, the jewel that "swings."

Nightlife

In Evening's Empire, *Craig Koslofsky describes how quickly the French court extended its events into the nighttime. Henry III (assassinated in 1589) had his last meal at six and was in bed by eight whereas, a century later, Louis XIV's official day didn't end until midnight. During his reign, all the major events — ballets de cour, operas, balls, masquerades, and fireworks, everything except hunting — took place at night. Nightlife was associated with luxury and revelry for the wellborn. Great spaces were built for balls, and status and attractiveness shone forth on the night stage. Women responded by wearing makeup, especially rouge on their cheeks and lips and black on their eyebrows, and diamond earrings. If a party went on until the wee hours, a person could expect to return home safely, after street lighting was introduced in Paris in 1667 (the first city in Europe to accomplish this).*

Charles Beaubrun, *Madame de Monpensier* (second half of 17th century).
Source: Alinari, Art Resource, New York.

Eighteenth Century:
Illuminating the Ear

> " *Qui sait ce que un bijou peut avoir dans l'âme?*
> *(Who can say what a gem has in its soul?)* "
>
> ~ Diderot

Jewelry of the beau monde shone with blinding extravagance in the eighteenth century. The girandole, set with gems or mirrored glass, was still composed of a mount, one large round gem or cluster, and three drops suspended below, but the arrangement became more rococo. For instance, a girandole might be assembled of several long pendants of precious and semi-precious stones in faceted rock crystal. Later in the century, looking like the gold leaf on cream or white walls and wallpaper, earrings resembled baskets of flowers and had the same curvilinear lines as the Louis XV furniture. Aristocratic women wore the pendeloques now instead of a single pendant, several in a cascade. Being lighter, the pendeloques could be longer and would mostly replace girandoles by century's end. When Pietro Longhi painted a playful game in 1744, in *The Simulated Faint*, the girl is wearing girandoles (a mere 1/16" on the canvas) that I associate with more formal attire. However, in a companion picture, *A Game of the Cooking Pot*, the girls are wearing pendeloques and they, too, look very fancy to romp in.

Antonio Amorosi, *Girl Sewing* (1720). Source: Museo Thyssen-Bornemisza, Madrid.

France

Diamonds became the *ne plus ultra* of gems for earrings in the courts of Europe. A diamond dazzles, but you can't look into it. Close to the level of the eyes, a diamond says, "I gaze at you, but you can't penetrate me," making it the supremely haughty earring jewel. Because Paris led in jewelry fashions during this era, the French term *parure* is a universal term for a set, coming from *apparâitre*, or to appear, as in "keeping up appearances." In the eighteenth century, a parure usually consisted of a necklace, earrings, and a brooch, and if just earrings and necklace, it was a *demi-parure*. The other term used for parure, "suite," also describes a type of instrumental music that Wolfgang Mozart wrote, with segments in the same key, but contrasting in rhythm or mood — and thus aptly pieces of jewelry that go together.

During a ball at court, ladies displayed their finest stones on their ears. Crystal-cut chandeliers became their most extravagant after the English developed lead glass in the seventeenth century. Adding lead made the glass refractory, so the tiers of flickering candles

Portuguese gold and silver. Source: Ouriversaria Antige de Jose Baptista.

Design for Aigrettes, 18th century drawing.
Source: Victoria & Albert Museum, London, UK/
Bridgeman Art Library.

reflected in the lighting fixture's pendants, sending rainbows in the halls. Wax candles could burn for hours, and sconces, glass chandeliers, and mirrors magnified their light... Earrings flashed.

Wealthy women were out on their own shopping in elegant boutiques in Paris and London. They gathered in salons. For daywear, they often wore paste jewels — basically what we call rhinestones. The effect on earrings was vast.

Through most of the seventeenth century, wood had been used for glass furnaces in England. However, the English needed timber for ships (marking all the tall conifers with the king's symbol riled the people of my state of Maine to revolutionary fervor), therefore burning wood to make glass was forbidden. In its place, coal, less clean-burning, was used and now glass melt had to be covered... Serendipity: the lead oxide added to reduce the higher melting point of coal, compared with wood, resulted in fine lead glass.

Hard and brilliant, the leaded glass could be cut and polished like a gem. It was Georges Frederic Stras, an Alsatian jeweler in Paris, who saw the virtue of the hard, brilliant lead glass for jewelry, although it was more difficult to cut than precious gems. Stras used mixtures of bismuth and thallium to improve the refractive quality of his imitations and produced different tints with metal

Anton Raphael Mengs, *Marie Louise de Parma*.
Source: Louvre, Erich Lessing, Art Resource, New York.

Italian provincial hoops, rose gold and silver, accented with rose cut diamonds.
Source: The Three Graces.

salts. The imitations were foil-backed and later given a mirror coating to add to their shimmer. He opened his business in 1730 and it was only four years later awarded the title of "King's Jeweler."

Picture the hard paste, made of ground glass, cut in facets like precious stones and with the foil glued to the backs to heighten the glitter — Stras paste sparkled like real diamonds. Grinding the glass was a meticulous craft and only the wealthy could afford paste. In movies, the beautiful noblewoman and her servant travel in a coach, with her lockbox of jewelry, and the handsome highwayman intercepts her passage. Sometimes the women wore little hinged orbs over the diamonds, and traveled with only their paste to foil the thieves. Paste, while expensive, was not valuable enough to risk one's neck. Aristocrats beat a path to the door of Stras's shop on the Quai des Orfèvres. By 1767, a corporation of *bijoutiers-faussetiers*, or costume jewelers, had over three hundred members in Paris. If something is good, more is better, and abundance is just right as costume jewelry proved.

Of Stras, *Maitre Orfèvre et Joaillier privilegié au Roi,* the 1740 *Dictionnaire de l'Académie Francaise,* stated: "In ten years, Stras had made his way, everyone knew him, women benefited from his brilliance, and his name passed into the language." Earrings by Stras were both refractive and wearable. Pigment could be added to tint glass to any desired color, and the glass could be cut into intricate designs. The very thin metal that lined the cups of paste were colorless for silver and gold for colored paste.

Paste jewelry came in many variations. By using paste, a goldsmith could have exact pear forms to go under ribbon bows. In Venice, turquoise pastes were a specialty. The English made colorless lead glass. The French put semi-opaque glass over pink foil, called opaline paste. Madame du Barry, renowned for her gems, also legitimized costume jewelry when she wore blue paste earrings, and Marie Antoinette bought paste at Au Petit Dunkerque.

MADAME DE POMPADOUR

King Louis XV (1710–74) was restless. His queen, Marie, had borne him ten children and was tired of him in her bed. The court looked for a mistress for the melancholic king. Valets sang the praise of a refined Parisian beauty, which piqued the king's curiosity. Jeanne-Antoinette Poisson (1721–1764) had the good fortune to come from a solid and stable family. Her grandfather was a weaver and her father acted as steward to prominent financiers. When she was nine, a fortune-teller predicted she would be the king's mistress; after that her family called her "Reinette." She received a private education in Paris, and was the habitué of literary salons, until she married up, to a man who was "nobility of the robe." Before she met Louis, Reinette had her own salon attended by luminaries such as Voltaire and Montesquieu.

Everyone can relate to the charming way the king and Jeanne-Antoinette first met — that Louis might surreptitiously see the reputed beauty she was invited to a winter masked ball in the Hall of Mirrors, her husband conveniently away in the south. Louis manufactured a disguise of eight yew trees for seven men and himself. The procession of them, clipped in the shape of pillars with vases, just like the topiaries in the chateau's park, entered, and he had a tryst with the masked beauty. At the end of several days of festivities, Jeanne-Antoinette was installed as mistress. Louis made her a marquise, although in history we know her as "Madame de Pompadour." Louis was known for a revolving door of mistresses, *des amours de passage*, but Madame de Pompadour stayed for twenty years. She loved the king and shared his interest in building and governing. Of Louis's passion for de Pompadour, a courtier, the Duc de Luynes, wrote:

> *As soon as the King is dressed, he goes down*
> *to Mme de Pompadour's; he stays with her until*
> *he goes to mass; after mass he goes back to her*

*and eats soup and a chop, for His Majesty does
not have a real dinner. [When he isn't hunting]
he stays there until five or six, when he attends
to business. On Council days, he visits her before
and after. Everybody tells me they find Mme de
Pompadour extremely polite. She is not nasty, she
doesn't say unpleasant things about people, she
doesn't even allow other people to do so. She is
cheerful and likes to talk. Far from being proud,
she continually refers to her family in the King's
presence.*

For the *grand couvert*, when the royal family dined
in public, Jeanne-Antoinette dressed in jewels and
formal clothes. She took the king to the seashore, flirted
with him in the mirrored Jardins d'Armide, and role-
played. She wore a variety of earrings to suit the occasion. In a painting by the rococo portraitist Maurice de
la Tour, she plays the shepherdess and wears gold hoops.
In Louise Vigée's portrait, de Pompadour wears big drop
pearls. (Vigée specialized in big, even shoulder-grazing
earrings, notably gold hoops with waterfalls, and oblong
pearls finished off with decorations of gold.) In François
Boucher's 1759 full-length portrait, she stands in a garden with her dog and wears round pearls (the Wallace
Collection, London), indicative of the financial security she had earned for herself and her family. Around
this time, de Pompadour paid off the queen's gambling
debts. She was firmly in the inner circle and could afford
to wear her choice of baubles.

A cut of diamonds developed by a royal jeweler,
which found its way into the repertoire of cuts for earrings, has the name "Marquise." Due to the long facets,
the marquise (also called *navette*, from the French,
or boat-shaped) is especially sparkly. Legend has it
that Louis asked the jeweler to create a diamond in the
shape of the mouth of his mistress. The "marquise"
shape is long and pointed at both ends, so it looks like
full, closed lips.

Francois Boucher, *Portrait of a Woman.*
Source: Pushkin Museum, Moscow, Bridgeman
Art Library.

MADAME DU BARRY

Jeanne Bécu (1743–93) became Louis XV's mistress
at age nineteen, when he was in his sixties, and Riche-
lieu was scouting around for a pretty girl to reawaken
the king's *joie de vivre*. She was a shop girl with a past,
and Louis had her married to a count, making her
Countess du Barry, so she could present at court. Louis
XV instructed the court bankers to accept du Barry's
drafts as orders from the king. She drew upon the treasury heavily for clothes, jewels, furniture, chandeliers,
and paintings. The king gave her jewels constantly, yet
she ran up immense bills on her own. She owned nearly
a thousand diamonds, as well as pearls, emeralds, sapphires, and gold jewelry.

At one fete, as Louis's consort, du Barry wore a green satin dress, with Flemish lace and wreaths of roses looped up with pearl earrings, valued at 12,000 livres. These verses at the theatrical performance during the fete were composed in her honor: *C'est la beauté qui nous mene a la verité.* (It's beauty that leads us to truth.)

Besides showering her with diamonds and other gems, the king gave her three properties in the town of Versailles and one four miles north — that was Louveciennes. There she was a patroness of artists and craftsmen and made Louveciennes a showplace, like a little Versailles. She was a faithful friend to the Enlightenment's most famous philosopher, Voltaire. Louise Vigée, who painted du Barry in her fifties, said she was easy-going and generous and not inclined to household management. Pastimes that most interested her were reading, dressing up (*à la toilette*) — she had the same dressmaker as Marie Antoinette — and her jewels. A group painting in the Louvre by Moreau le Jeune shows a party at Louveciennes in December 1771. Du Barry sits to the right of the king. Servants, ladies, and lords proliferate, and the king looks detached from the scene as he rests an arm on the table. Du Barry has on a white or pink gown. Her diamond earrings and necklace dazzle in the blazing light of chandeliers and torches.

Jewels mattered enormously to a mistress of the *ancien regime* because, unlike the chateaux, they were her own property to keep, sell, or bequeath as she wished. In her marriage contract with the Count du Barry, Madame du Barry kept the jewels she had received from previous protectors. She had an endless collection of necklaces, bracelets, rings, and earrings of diamonds and pearls, and her jeweler, Rouen, was constantly resetting them to suit the fashions.

After Louis XV died, in a sort of modified suttee, du Barry was removed from the court to a convent. Her lover, the Duc du Brissac, protected her and man-aged to reintroduce her to the court of Louis XVI, even though Marie Antoinette despised her. Du Brissac, for a time, was head of the *garde constitutionelle* under the revolutionary government, but remained a royalist at heart and eventually fell to the guillotine.

Worried that Louis XVI would confiscate gifts from the late king and impoverish her, du Barry had the court jeweler, Aubert, visit her and instructed him to sell her parure of diamonds and another parure of rubies and diamonds to pay off her debts. She hid them in a chest of drawers and writing desk in her bedroom. However, her valet, who was supposed to stand guard, took advantage of her being off in Paris at du Brissac's and got to the jewelry first. He and his accomplices took all the loot in a sack to Paris and sold it to a fence who was also in the watch trade.

Handbills offering a fair reward were distributed all over Paris and two very large diamond earrings led the list. However, the gang leader quickly melted the gold items and loosened the stones with nitric acid, and, feigning that he had the goods from Frenchmen who were expatriating, went to a respectable London businessman with the loot. This was a mistake. Arrests were made and the jewels confiscated; du Barry went to London to recover them, and dined with the Lord Mayor.

The case dragged on for months in British courts over who would receive the rewards. Du Barry hastened to Paris and returned, being careful to have her passports in order to avoid suspicion she was emigrating. (In Dickens' *The Tale of Two Cities*, this was what led to Charles Darnay's arrest.) Back in Louveciennes, she had the chest of drawers repaired and presumed the business would be settled soon, when the Duc de Brissac was arrested. Before he was executed, during months of imprisonment, he wrote du Barry: "I kiss you 1,000, 1,000 times. Yes, you will be my last thought." He bequeathed her his property for her life or cash in his will: "I ask her to accept this small pledge of my feelings and of my gratitude, being all the more in her debt because I was the unwilling cause of the loss of her diamonds."

The chancery court case still had to be settled in England when du Barry was imprisoned in Sainte-Pelagie. At the trial, she was accused of being an émigré, because of her several stays in London, and to have falsified the jewel theft. Ironically, her execution was delayed until evening while she drew up a list of jewels tucked away in the chateau and stolen jewels deposited in the English bank.

In 1795, the original Mr. James Christie himself auctioned the du Barry jewelry "of most singular excellence, beauty, and perfection," as the auction poster said.

MARIE ANTOINETTE
Naturally, Marie Antoinette (1755–1793) was a legendary jewelry hound, her favorite gems being pearls and diamonds. When she left Vienna at age 12, she abandoned her pup and her jewelry at the Austrian-French border, and in compensation received new French jewelry. When the dauphin was crowned Louis XVI, he gave Marie Antoinette a pair of girandoles with two pear-shaped brilliant-cut diamonds.

As queen of France, Marie Antoinette greatly exceeded her personal allowance. She bought an average of 170 gowns a year and a hairdresser came from Paris each day to arrange her hair into tall artifices. Someone sent her mother Marie-Therese in Vienna a sketch of her, and the Empress replied, "Is that the Queen of France or an actress? A Queen can only degrade herself by such impossible behavior and degrades herself even more by this sort of heedless extravagance, especially in difficult times… I hope I shall not live to see the disaster which is all too likely to occur." They were mere bagatelles to a queen.

In 1775, it was noted by a Mrs. Thrale that "There were no diamonds at all at Court but the Queen's ear-rings." Newly crowned, Marie Antoinette bought these in 1774 for herself. Next from the same jeweler, August Bohmer, she purchased a diamond spray and diamond bracelet, followed by chandelier earrings.

Pearls grew less popular when women began to wear white cotton dresses in the style of the French colonies where the cotton came from. Marie Antoinette, who did not like to be restrained, adopted the more relaxed style of dress when pregnant with her first child in 1778. It took the name *la chemise de la reine*. Gathered at the bodice, with ties over the sleeves, and decorated by a colored silk ribbon at the waist, the style, visible in many of Louise Vigee's paintings, represents a harbinger of the Revolution, a volte-face from the highly constructed gowns of society ladies before — except that abundant jewels went with it.

Two large pear-shaped diamonds, weighing about 14 and 21 carats, in the Smithsonian's Gem Gallery, once belonged to Marie Antoinette. They were reputedly her favorite pieces of jewelry. She had them in a jewel case when she tried to flee France. They were taken from her but they appeared to have stayed in the royal family. In 1853, Napoleon III gave Empress Eugenie a pair of earrings made from these large pear-shaped diamonds as a wedding gift. When the Second Empire collapsed, a Russian grand duchess acquired the diamonds. Pierre Cartier bought the diamond earrings in 1928 and described the settings as original. Bands of silver surrounded the pears, with gold linkages and decorated with old mine cut diamonds in scrollwork. The heiress to the cereal fortune, Marjorie Merriweather Post, purchased the earrings from Cartier a year later. Harry Winston reset them for her in platinum replicas of the original silver settings in 1959, and Cartier replaced the tops with new triangular diamonds set in platinum.

Spain

In Spain, women glittered from head to foot. Spanish women held tenaciously to the girandole style, creating many variations. In Goya's painting of a family, the mother tilts her head to show off her earrings, and the young daughter at her side has a fine pair too. The upper class Majas in Goya's painting of them on the balcony are dressing down, as if they are hataera, or classy mistresses. A woman who leaned over a balcony could show off her earrings to advantage. Since having an entire set of jewels was essential to girls, paste became especially popular in Spain. A ribbon and attachment loops, rather than ear wire, often fastened the earrings, which were still heavy compared with the style elsewhere.

England

Portraits of Mrs. Philip Thicknesse show the lady in rows of beads on her neck, bracelets on both hands, and big earrings. In the Gainsborough 1760 portrait, she wears gold with stones. Her dress is natural with cascading folds of white, balanced by the jewelry. Her aristocratic father went up in smoke when she decided to earn her living in the theater — he hired ruffians to interrupt her performances. Are we surprised she liked earrings?! The earring initiates what Hogarth called a two-dimensional "line of beauty" in the Gainsborough portrait — a spiraling movement that runs from the earring down the jaw-line to the right shoulder, arm, and leg. Like a star that is a point in a constellation, the earring begins a down and outward curve offset by upward converging diagonals of the dress. In 1771, Gainsborough depicted Frances, Countess of Dartmouth, with ropes of pearls and flower-petaled pearl earrings. In other portraits of Mrs. Thomas Matthews

and Miss Clarges of Richmond, the ladies wore short pearl necklaces and pearl-centered earbobs.

Charlotte, the wife of George III, was queen from 1761 to 1818, the longest reign of a queen at her time. From 1811, when George was declared mad, until her death, she was her husband's legal guardian. Charlotte had fifteen children, thirteen of whom survived to adulthood. An epistolary friend of Marie Antoinette, she kept apartments ready for the royal family of France, who did not come to their senses and lingered too long. Charlotte had the towering French-style powdered hair, but rather than gobs of jewels on her garments, she wore parures of necklaces, earrings, and bracelets, which have a modern look. Her son, George IV, claimed her jewels as his personal legacy at her death.

The prize for the most ostentatious diamonds goes to Charlotte. The earrings, seen in another Gainsborough painting, are pendeloques, and the absolutely colorless diamonds, from India, had their own name, the Arcot diamonds, a gift from the Nawab of Arcot, who presented them to Queen Charlotte in 1777. By 1959, when Harry Winston purchased the Arcot diamonds, they figured in a tiara. Charlotte was believed to have had an African forebear, and apparently Sir Allen Ramsey, a strong anti-slavery intellectual, painted her to show off that heritage. The diamond earrings, while exceedingly large, look regal on Charlotte. They have large, round tops and the big Arcot teardrops suspended from a diamond-encrusted bow. In a portrait by Johan Zoffany, Charlotte is at ease, wearing discs in her ears covered with pearls.

The English favored a relaxed style of dress with less girding and rigging during the eighteenth century. With it came a vogue for semi-precious stones, including garnets, coral, and rock crystal, which meant fancy earrings were more widely affordable. Theater-going gave earrings another boost. In the Georgian playhouse, people of all classes came to see a spectrum of entertainment, from pantomime to tightrope walking. The auditorium was almost as brightly lit as the stage, showing earrings to good effect. In this republican atmosphere, with well-known female actresses dressed in current styles, characters like rakes and courtesans often mocked the aristocrats. George Cruickshank satirized lounging ladies with tasteless garb and oversized plumes and long pendeloque earrings.

Earrings were decorated with scrollwork and ornate motifs, and the girandole style continued to predominate. In Boston's Museum of Fine Arts is a pair of English girandoles made of *coque de perle*, a pearl-like stone cut from the Indian nautilus shell and resembling a blister pearl. The earrings are comprised of five well-defined plump ovals: the top two horizontal, two verticals attached to finely wrought gold leaves, and the central, bottom one extending down.

Russia

Russian goldsmiths were ever-outstanding and, during this period, Saint Petersburg was a capital of impressive and costly adornment. A favorite daughter of Peter the Great, Elisabeth Petrovna ruled Russia for twenty years after she engineered a bloodless coup. She had access to the jewel vaults of the Kremlin and the "Diamond Room" of the Winter Palace. At her coronation, she wore with her golden gown what antiquarian sellers in France call *des bijoux importants,* earrings with enamel-framed, big gems hanging from thick gold discs. Elisabeth loved parties, galas, and masquerade balls. She was known to change her dress (with new suites of jewels to match) four or five times during Winter Palace dances. At her death, 5,000 gowns, all worn only once, were in her wardrobe.

Elisabeth reigned during the period of the rococo taste. Rococo was invented in France, but quickly swept all of Europe with its ebullient and frivolous style. The rococo embraced organic forms, such as flowers, garlands, animals, rock formations, and the flow of water. My favorite are Elisabeth's earrings in the form of garlands of flowers with bees crawling over them, which have traveled from Russia to America in a collection of Romanov jewelry. The bee-motif earrings are remarkable. The Indian diamonds were slightly different colors, set with foil to reflect pale pastels that are not the actual colors of the stones. The uneven clarities are corrected by the addition of color, causing the stones to appear as if they are rare fancy yellow, pink, or blue diamonds. A friend of mine calls them "Jordan Almonds" due to their colors of pistachio green, pale pink, and mellow yellow. Elisabeth's jeweler, perhaps one of the many French, German, or Swiss who flocked to St. Petersburg to make their fortunes, used a technique called *"en tremblant,"* in which the components are mounted on tiny springs and wires. The bees flutter and the flowers move.

Two other pairs of earrings in the Romanov collection — ruby earrings in the form of cascades and sapphire earrings inspired by the fountains at St. Petersburg's Peterhof Palace — also had moving elements likely to mesmerize anyone seeing a woman wearing them turn her head. This jewelry was meant to move, which is precisely why they embody the fluttering, frivolous, fanciful rococo spirit.

Empress Elisabeth gave her daughter-in-law, the German princess Catherine (soon-to-be the Great), her choice of jewels at her wedding. Catherine lacked the beauty of her husband Peter's great love and mistress, Anna Mons, but her coronation was awash in jewels and she was soon wearing magnificent girandoles with several types of gemstones.

America

In eighteenth century America, women wore earrings from abroad or styled after European pairs. Only freshwater pearls from American rivers were indigenous. Sea pearls were imported from the Persian Gulf and the Indian Ocean while faux pearls came from France. In the eighteenth century, the *Virginia Gazette* had advertisements for wax pearl earrings. This may have meant the ingenious fake pearls that Maître Jacquin developed in Paris early in the century. He coated hollow balls of blown glass with a mixture of varnish and fish scales, and filled them with wax. He developed his formula in order to make his daughter-in-law's betrothal jewelry, and women loved his fake pearls because they were the most durable and lustrous.

Young ladies wore all manner of earrings: seed pearls, cut-steel (with its potential for minute faceting, it saw its heyday late in the century), jet, enamel, paste, and especially garnets (the stones from Bohemia or Perignan in the foothills of the Pyrenees). In 1774, the advertisements of a New York jeweler, Charles Bruff, in the *New York Gazette* ran as follows: "At the sign of the tea-pot, tankard, and ear-ring, between Maiden Lane and Crown Street." Pictured are a buckle, ring, seal fob, and diamond girandoles.

George Washington bought a garnet necklace for his bride, Martha, in 1759. The next year, he ordered from another London jeweler a pair of "3 drop garnet earrings." They were girandoles with a rosette surmount and three pear pendants suspended from a bowknot. It's lovely to think of our most revered founding father busy supplying earrings for a lady.

Some slaves in America had holiday clothes they wore on Sunday, at funerals, and at Christmas, when they had days off. Slave owners tried to restrain them from dressing fancy, but there are records of their using

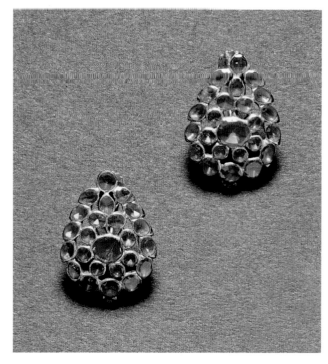

Gold, silver, garnet, made by J. Grymes, retailed in London, England (1760).
Source: George Washington's Mount Vernon Estate, Museum & Gardens.

Fray Miguel de Herrera, *Portrait of a Lady*.
Source: Museo Franz Mayer Mexico, Gianni Dagli Orti, Art Resource, New York.

John Durand, Mrs. Thomas
Newton, Jr. (Martha Tucker),
Virginia (c. 1770).
Source: The Colonial Williamsburg
Foundation. Gift of M. Knoedler and
Company, Inc.

their small cash sums (we are surprised they were paid anything) to buy colorful dresses and silver bobs for their ears and, in the case of a South Carolinian slave, silver drops for her daughter. Ads for runaways are a heart-stopping source for this kind of information. Striped gown, silver buckles, and silver bobs might be the attire of a runaway slave from the South, although the more typical suit was the one assigned to field slaves of a waistcoat and matching petticoat.

Designs and objects of adornment were traded internationally. In *Jewelry in America, 1600–1900*, Martha Gandy Fales reveals the similarities between what a young Virginia Algonquin man wore on his ears in 1645 (in an etching by Wenceslaus Hollar) to what a Southern Colonial woman was wearing a century later. The freshwater pearl cluster earrings and necklaces look so much alike with their triangular fan pendants that they might as well be the same pair!

In an oval miniature, a Virginia merchant's daughter, married at thirteen to a plantation owner, wears two miniatures in the miniature: one of a woman at her throat with the double strand pearl choker and another of a man pinned to her bodice. A tall, white curling feather rises over her head, attached to a headband of white ribbons and pearls. She is Fannie Hipkins Bernard, with dark brown hair and blue eyes and wearing drop pearl earrings. She lived in Belle Grove Plantation in the Shenandoah Valley, now a bed-and-breakfast and the birthplace of James Madison. Patently, colonial and federalist Americans imported many luxuries from Europe, but that some wore earrings like those on ladies strolling in Vauxhall Gardens seems a revelation.

Sweetmeat stand, faceted glass and gilt
metal, English (c. 1760).
Source: The Colonial Williamsburg Foundation. Gift of
Mr. John V. Rowan, Jr. in memory of Winifred Draco
Shrubsole.

Georgian diamonds.
Source: Exceptional Vintage.

Pearl, mother of pearl, silver (1789).
Source: George Washington's Mount Vernon Estate,
Museum & Gardens.

The French Empire: **Pampering** Josephine

" *A thing of beauty is a joy for ever:*
Its loveliness increases; it will never
Pass into nothingness. "

~ John Keats

Guillotines

On display in the Carnavalet Museum in Paris hang *à la guillotine* earrings. They consist of a tiny guillotine, with a bonnet of liberty on top and a pendant below in the form of two decapitated heads; on one earring the king's and on the other the queen's. Who wore these macabre ornaments?

The guillotine was the stage for grisly public theater. Like Charles Dickens' fictional Madame Defarge, *tricoteuses*, women knitters, sat beneath the execution platform. They began chanting as the tumbril arrived, and cheered each chopped head, all the while knitting. They wore tricolor badges or rosettes...but guillotine earrings? Probably not. These spectators were peasants and unaccustomed to bearing witness by jewels dangling from their ears. More likely, the women who wore the earrings were shopkeepers and bourgeois wives. Like tricolor striped skirts and nosegays, or jewelry set with chunks from the Bastille, the guillotines testified to a person's daring (unmistakably they were symbols of castration) and being on the winning side. Other Revolutionary memorials included red ribbons, which young people festooned to their necks as they danced at a *bal de victimes*, jerking their heads to their chests instead of bowing to mimic decapitation.

It might be that these earrings graced women's ears as the Revolution subsided, when its horrors were less vivid. In this case, the earrings miniaturized and reduced the scale of the nightmare, putting a nostalgic distance between the wearers and the terrible events. Strangely enough, even though we now associate the guillotine with bloody executions, Joseph Guillotin invented the apparatus as a humane alternative to the axe and hanging. The tiny, neatly crafted guillotines suggested egalitarianism of a new society even at the cost of 17,000 executions of fellow citizens.

France: Earrings with guillotine, from the time of the French Revolution. Anonymous. Source: Objet d'art. Paris, Musee Carnavalet. © Michel Toumazet Musée Carnavalet Roger-Viollet. The Image Works.

Rustics and Poissards

During and immediately after the Revolution, simple attire was politically correct and practical. Wars, famines, and the aristocrats' siphoning off wealth had severely reduced France's standard of living. Precious riches also bought expatriate aristocrats new lives abroad. The neo-classical style of dress and the state of people's purse meant light earrings. In portraits from the Revolution, ladies wore hoops like country folk and designs inspired by jewelry recovered from the ruins of Pompeii. Women didn't want to look like nobles so they began imitating the women and goddesses of Greek mythology. On their ears they wore cameos of Artemis, Athena, and the standard Roman general. The rococo, "with its hedonistic and licentious overtones, its *fetes galantes* and scenes of casual dalliance suggestive of the boudoir and feminine voluptuousness," (Hugh Honour, *Neo-Classicism*) fell from favor with a jolt. Revolutionary women of fashion exhibited the homely virtues and heroic values touted by the new regime in contrast to the self-indulgence of discarded monarchy and aristocracy.

Poissardes.
Source: Amanda Grove Holmen.

During the first stable government after the Revolution, the French Directory (1795–99), women wore filmy dresses, low-cut with a ribbon around a high waist. They sometimes bathed in these dresses before going to a ball to create the ultimate in clinginess. They wore chignons with curls around the forehead, rings, bracelets, and, on their ears, *poissardes*, "fishwives" or long earrings, often with two or three geometric motifs, or gems, one below the other on its flattened ellipse. The fitting behind the ear made a big loop from top to bottom, resembling a fishhook, and it closed back to front, at the top.

This unusual style had a rip-roaring history. Ever since medieval kings gave poor women the privilege of selling fish in Les Halles, the old market of Paris, the *poissardes*, or women fishmongers, constituted a renegade of free-wheeling sensibility. The market women must have been an eye-catching sight, selling colorful fish while wearing bright silks and laces. Their spicy slang and elongated, drooping earrings were part of the show. Several times a year, the king invited the market women of Les Halles to Versailles. Their presence at a royal wedding symbolized to the king the support of the Third Estate. For the king to have the friendship of the women who sold the fish, which was prescribed for all of Lent, was of practical importance; however, this popularity slowly eroded until he lost it entirely. In 1787, the *poissardes* boycotted the festivities of the Feast of the Assumption when they were expected to give Marie Antoinette flowers and compliments. The *coup de grace* came when the price of bread soared in the fall of 1789. Intoxicated with revolution, the fishmongers of Les Halles marched to Versailles on October 5th, confronted the king, and the next day forced the royal family to decamp for

virtual imprisonment in Paris — the true beginning of the end of the *ancien regime*.

To wear *poissardes* in the decades that followed had to echo the vitality of the rough and ready businesswomen who wore them first. Although no pictures of the original earrings are available, it is possible to tease out something of *poissardes* as the market women first wore them. First of all, the S-bar held the jewelry on better than the simple hook, and these businesswomen had a very active day. Also, there is a shield-like look to how three or so motifs go down the rigid front part all in a line; the effect is of a row of buttons on a coat. Adding to the sturdiness, an extra eye on the wire either stops the earring from moving, or was tied in the hair.

Approximately through the rule of Napoleon, a vogue continued for these longer earrings accentuating metal, whether all metal or with seed pearls and colored stones, and therefore sensible when fine gems were scarce. Even the fasionistas, called *merveilleuses*, wore *poissardes*. I light up when I see a pair of *poissardes* illustrated or for sale, partly because of their distinction — airy, yet imposing and masterworks often of the jeweler's craft — and partly because I think of the market women. *Cocarde* derives from "cock," and the market women, walking tall and arrogant, with rosettes in their hair and *poissardes* in their ears, took the lead for the men and the people of Paris to overthrow oppression. The market women could have struck down the king at Versailles, but they wanted only justice for their families; in the mass violence that ensued, the *poissarde* earrings are untarnished.

The face of jewelry was no longer the aristocrat with her diamonds. As diamonds and gold were in short supply, the field leveled: jewelry of silver and marcasite, brass hoops, and artificial pearls exemplified a type of jewelry within the pocketbook of many citizens, resulting in a wave of adornment across Europe and America. Now, the middle-class lady was spending time at her ritual toilette. She wore few cosmetics (no more lead powder) and focused on just the right jewels. Olivier Bernier, in his *The World In 1800*, tells the story of a German composer who visited a lady to

relatives. Napoleon's *corbeille* to Marie-Louise had twelve dozen each of every kind of undergarment, as well as costly jewels — emerald and opal parures, everyday jewelry of lapis lazuli, coral and steel, and other personal items bespeaking her new status as imperial consort. As fashion was now an established fact, the groom was inclined to present his wife-to-be with loose jewels that she could have set as she chose. Goodbye to hoops, bustles and corsets...for a generation.

Marie-Louise bore Napoleon a son, but hardly had time to enjoy her famous ruby and diamond parures as the Empire fell in 1814, after only four years of marriage. Under the Restoration, Louis XVIII had the gems partially reset in a style reminiscent of Marie Antoinette's jewelry. A central emerald briolette (pear-shaped) drop is suspended from the point of the mount, a square emerald. Tiny round diamonds surround the mount. The briolette hangs free, but is surrounded by a loop of gold wire mounted with large rose cut diamonds and a round emerald at the bottom of the hoop.

While he ruled as emperor, Napoleon wanted all the women of his family to shine brilliantly at court occasions, so Nitot and other top jewelers received many commissions from members of the Bonaparte clan. Napoleon's female relatives can be viewed in portraits where they are decked in the jewels he gave to or provided for them. Artists found these easy subjects, an impressive garb making for an impressive painting, all the way up the scale to David's ermine robes and crown. My vote for the one who looks both stately and pretty in her jewels is Hortense, Napoleon's stepdaughter by Josephine. She married Louis, one of Napoleon's brothers, and became queen of Holland. She remained devoted to her stepfather after he divorced Josephine, and became mother to Napoleon III, whom she infused with ideas of greatness when he was a boy. In a portrait by Regnault at Malmaison, she wears a tiara, necklace, armband-style bracelets, and long, two-drop earrings.

Hortense wanted to be educated and accomplished. She choreographed a ballet-skit in the winter of 1811 for a masked ball. Two dozen priestesses of the sun surrounded Hortense as the high priestess. Napoleon raved, "You're so brilliant! I can't look at you!" "I would be quite a prize as I am now, covered with diamonds," demurred Hortense, but Napoleon replied, "You know very well the best diamond without price is the person inside the costume."

Jerome Bonaparte's wife, the Princess of Wurtemburg, wore emerald earrings set in diamonds with big pearl pendants for a portrait by Gerard in 1807. Family members, like his sister Pauline, wore the total parure, including tiaras, earrings, and necklaces for portraits, all the more prominent due to the simple drapery of their gowns.

In Marie-Guillemine Benoîst's 1805 portrait of Napoleon's most interesting sibling, Elisa Bonaparte, Elisa has the family resemblance around the eyes and mouth. She is dressed in a feminine gold-on-white satin brocade gown and wears a tiara and drop earrings, dispensing with necklace or other gems. She rests one arm on a gold swan armrest. She turns her own head like a swan, so one sparking of white shines on the side against a dark background while another is a mere sparkle. On some of the ruling class, evidenced in their portraits, the jewelry looked like cold armor, but Elisa's earrings glow as she seems to adjust her posture for the artist.

Benoîst started to paint with Elisabeth Vigee Le Brun and entered the studio of David. Her naturalistic style made jewelry look part of a woman's personality. She also painted an important image for women's emancipation and the rights of black people, *Portrait d'une Négresse*, exhibited in 1800. This was painted six years after the Directorate abolished slavery in 1794. The willowy elegant woman, a model from Guadeloupe, has a white turban and gold hoops that accentuate her dark skin. To the French of that time, the portrait conjured up national pride. She was beautiful and so was Guadeloupe, for which they had traded their possessions in Canada in the mid-eighteenth century.

Pauline Borghese, another sister to Napoleon, also favored very long pearl drops. Her husband had her sculpted by Canova in the semi-nude, which was risqué for a person of high position. "How could she?" Pauline was asked. She quipped that a stove in the studio kept her warm. In a portrait, Pauline wears a tiara, headband, and big, round, classically-inspired earrings, almost like big emblems. She certainly saw herself as a latter day Roman princess, and the earrings are part of the show.

JUST PEARLS

Above all others, the most celebrated beauty of her age was probably Juliette Recamier (1777–1849), who epitomizes the less is more approach to jewelry. She wore only white gowns and pearls — the finest to be found — as her husband, Jacques Recamier, was an important and exceedingly rich banker. Juliette refused to be a lady in waiting at the imperial court and refused to sleep with Napoleon's brother. For these dual offenses, Napoleon likely manipulated the failure of Jacques's banking enterprise. It is said that Jacques was in fact Juliette's mother's lover and that the marriage (in 1793) was a ruse so that she could inherit his property if he were guillotined. Juliette lived an irreproachable life, which, although she had lots of jewelry, was advertised by the pearls on her ears and wrists.

Lacy Metal Dangles

Now we go to Prussia, today's Germany/Poland, and an early, very successful factory production of earrings, which converged with a government's involvement in what women wore in their ears.

Fer de Berlin had a blitz of fashion. Women in Europe, Russia, and America wore intricate but modest black jewelry with their high-waisted, white sheaths. A beautiful and popular young Prussian queen, Luise, introduced the Grecian-style dresses, shocking the court, and, during the years of oppression, when Napoleon occupied the land, she wore black iron jewelry, a novelty with a political message, as the royal family called on Prussia's large middle class to exchange their gold jewelry for cast-iron. Earrings bore the scaled down design emblem of an iron cross like what Teutonic knights wore.

Iron jewelry began in 1798 when the director of one of the royal foundries returned from England with reliefs and glass pastes of Wedgwood, which were reproduced in iron casts to produce medallions. By molding the medallions, the ironworks became adept at casting very small intricate parts. A most famous neo-classical designer of the casts, Karl Friedrich Schinkel, made designs for bridge railings before dabbling in jewelry, and went on to build Berlin's notable Palace Bridge and immense Altes Museum. The iron jewelry parts were cast after brass or silver examples. To produce the many small parts, a method was developed where the tiny molds were connected to casting "trees." After the casting, the jewelry was polished and several layers of thin lacquer applied, and dried.

In 1808, a French General requisitioned models from the foundry, including over seven hundred jewelry molds, which he sent to a Paris foundry that Napoleon established. However, Berlin continued as the center for the paper-thin iron jewelry, which is credited to the skill of the mold-makers and the fine sand that came from the Brandenburg region. The iron had a trace of phosphorus that allowed intricate pieces to be cast, which were then assembled into the desired piece

Biennais Martin-Guillaume. Jewelry Case of Empress Josephine (1802–04).
Source: RMN-Grand Palais Art Resource, New York.

Miniature Portrait of Fannie Hipkins Bernard (1800–01).
Source: The Colonial Williamsburg Foundation. Museum Purchase.

of jewelry. The cast-iron earrings, in contrast to what the name suggests, were light as a feather.

During the devastating Seven Years War, Louis XV's finance minister had also called upon the French to donate gems in exchange for metal of little value, cut-steel. However, the cast-iron jewelry, unlike cut-steel, could be mass-produced. Besides, the drive to vanquish Napoleon built up for two unhappy decades. When, after the Battle of Waterloo, numerous countries banded together and forced his abdication, cast-iron jewelry peaked in popularity.

In 1814, more than 40,000 pieces left the Royal Ironworks, and Berlin had many other foundries that exported iron jewelry. After 1815, the neo-classical motifs (e.g., acanthus leaves, rosettes, palmettos) ceded to neo-Gothic tracery decoration — pointed arches and trefoils, quatrefoils, and luxurious vines, like wrought-iron gates. As the fashion for *fer de Berlin* waned, the Royal Ironworks stopped casting jewelry and some firms tried to introduce new shapes, like earrings of rolled iron wire, that resembled springs of box mattresses. During the early 1800s, it was beautiful.

Beyond the Empire

The empire style traveled to America. A few months before her marriage on June 2, 1812, Frances Bragg and her husband-to-be had their half-length portraits painted. She wears a flimsy "Wendy" white dress, embroidered with tiny dots and having a square, low neckline, short puffed sleeves, and a high, Empire-style satin belt. She has dark ringlets and her only jewelry is the gold clasp on her belt and her drop earrings, which are, according to Janine E. Skerry, Curator of Metals at Williamsburg, probably of the detachable type, given their size. One earring, visible on her right ear, is suspended from a gold wire, with a large, round stone or paste hanging below. The stone is faceted, edged with seed pearls, and a pendant pearl drop hangs below the round stone. Her adornment is surely the height of elegance and our stereotype of a woman of means in the early republic must be

Source: Jane Merrill.

adjusted accordingly. The portrait registers a precious moment in Frances's life of radiant happiness, while dark clouds form the background. The next year, shortly after the birth of their child, her husband James, a Norfolk merchant, was lost at sea, and she lived her life out with her adult daughter and son-in-law.

Romanticism: 1815–1840

" *Ich gab Gold für eissen. (I gave gold for iron.)* "

~ Early 1800s inscription on Berlin Iron jewelry

I choose to call the early nineteenth century "Romantic" because this period featured gallant swains, heaving bosoms, and evocative, sometimes imposing jewelry. It was a magnificent period for earrings, in part because of a shortage of gold. There was manufacture, but wearing earrings was still beyond the pocket of most women, so having them whispered the possibility they came from a lover. In his last play, Georg Buchner, a German writing in Zurich, hangs all the tragic *crime passionel* of how the poor barber sees an earring flash in the hand of his common-law wife. When he comes in, she jumps up, hands to her ears.

This period of great artistry saw an extensive fashion for earrings that did not match: little sculptures, cameos where complementary profiles or corresponding scenes, graced each ear. Jewelers, inspired by antique earrings unearthed in the ancient civilizations of Egypt and Etrusca, created cameos and engraved gems. The Royal Collection in London has early nineteenth century pendants with late nineteenth century settings that epitomize the attraction of the cameos. One cameo shows figures shearing sheep — the male figure sits astride the sheep to hold it in place and the female figure holds another sheep on her lap to shear it. On another cameo, a nude male figure carrying a net is attempting to capture a bird. The small scale of these cameos astonishes us. They are carved just like a sculpture, and crafted with extreme delicacy. The best cameos, showing heads or busts, reveal character, and the ghostly dreaminess of the earrings with the sheep tableaux are emotionally touching. It's like looking into the scene in a blown-out egg decorated for Easter.

I remember studying my mother's cameos (along with kid gloves and sterling silver that later made my family sick because of the alloy), which she bought when we were in Naples in the early 1950s. The images were so romantic — the cameos had movement and yet stayed the same, like a movie still.

Day-Night Cameos.
Source: Jane Merrill.

The Romantics liked cameos engraved from hard stones and shells. A shell is a natural souvenir and this was a great age for touring and travel. Romantics put a shell to their ears to understand the mysteries of the universe. In William Turner's 1817 painting of the eruption of Vesuvius, a sky rages with atmosphere and intuitive color so that it looks like chalcedony or veined yellow quartz. The young Turner created a sensation with his surging, visual emotions and in jewelry women wore gems in colors of fire and water, including peridot, citrine, aquamarine, garnet, and heat-treated topaz. After Vesuvius, lava became another material for cameos. Diamond earrings were smaller stones because being set in silver they had to be lighter. The designs showed the gems as ostentatiously as possible.

Christine Belgioioso

Christine Belgioioso, an Italian aristocrat, scholar, and political activist, lived in exile in Paris from 1830 to 1847. There, she hosted a salon that attracted such luminaries as De Tocqueville, Liszt, Balzac, and Lafayette, as well as Italian revolutionaries. This radical feminist married at sixteen, separated amicably from her husband soon after, had many lovers, and a child (by whom no one is sure), and wore gorgeous earrings. She was said to be the richest heiress in Italy, although she lived in relative modesty close to the Madeleine in Paris. In a stunning portrait, the Italian painter Francesco Hayez shows her looking self-confident in her allure, very fetching and intense. She is wearing a kind of girandole that was briefly in vogue at that period, *coque de perle*, whose thick luster accentuates the brightness of her nature. Each element of the earrings is the mother-of-pearl "coque" of a single snail (from the East Indies), which is filled underneath and then set, like mabe blister pearls.

Georgian: the Antiquarian Term

The term Georgian is often used for jewelry of the Romantic period. This seems to be because, where jewelers congregated, the name follows. France had suffered ravages of the imperial wars, so many jewelers, including royalists and Huguenots, moved to England. Look at the scrolls on Chippendale furniture, or fountains and gardens by Capability Brown, and you see the same designs as earrings of that same period. This was also the time of the English regency and rule of the last of the four Georges. George IV himself had a passion for lavish jewels.

Francesco Hayez, *Cristina Belgioioso*.
Source: Cameraphoto Arte, Venice,
Art Resource, New York.

EXQUISITE CRAFT

At night, wearing perhaps a little ribbon around her neck and an expanse of bare shoulders, a lady paid attention to her earrings, large or small. It was fashionable to wear a voluminous dress and finely wrought earrings, fewer diamonds than semi-precious stones set *en cabochon*, often with closed-back mountings, and light designs, in advance of the discovery of gold in America. Earrings were crafted with filigree, piercing work, and a new kind of gold work called "cannetille" of fine twisted wires dotted with gold granules, named after a type of Neapolitan embroidery. Two pairs of my earrings from this period sound hollow and feel marvelously light. They are repoussé, or hand-hammered, with some of the black lines and curlicues stamped mechanically. Others have aquamarine set in gold leaves and cornelian, which feels outstandingly romantic.

Georgian garnets (1820).
Source: Glorious Antique Jewelry.

In 1819, the Duke of Kent gave the Duchess a portrait of her daughter (his stepchild) Feodora. She wears high, braided hair and spit curls around her face. You can see the neo-Classical traces morphing into Romantic, and the earrings are pearls hanging from a diamond-shaped mount of small gems. The Duchess, in her picture by the same artist, George Dawe, wears a parure of great delicacy, from tiara and earrings to three tiered pearls and bracelet. She has a look of Josephine grown-up, with her dark gown edged with a whisper of fine lace around the neckline and the cap sleeves. Striking is her deep décolletage, which was fashionable in the 1820s to the 1840s. With the expanse of shoulders uncovered for the fancy evening wear, women liked to have their earrings richly decorative, with all sorts of flowers, leaves, wreaths, and ribbons as motifs.

Jewelry was also beloved for long matte gold or coral drops and girandoles with lapis lazuli or coral drops. Motifs included amphora and ears of wheat, with tiny colored gems like garnets on bright gold. A characteristic and graceful style was the long torpedo shaped drop. This could either be a carved gemstone like chalcedony, niello-work or all gold filigree.

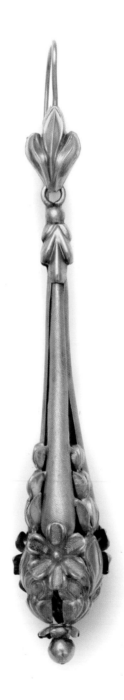

Georgian gold torpedoes.
Source: Glorious Antique Jewelry.

TORPEDOS

I stress a *je ne sais quoi* tactile appeal of Romantic earrings: the dramatic torpedo drops, up to four inches, of carved or set gemstones, or worked all in gold feel cool and feminine. These lighter hollow-backed earrings clack and feel terrific. Why? Because they are lighter than they look. To offset the broad clothes and necklines, jewelers made these astonishing earrings. The very size gave them space to do pique, or the metal hammered, to the front (repousse), and Near Eastern pique, coils of cannetille, and other textural effects. Yet, for all their assertiveness, no strings tied them to the hair to wear them. They fluttered and swayed. I especially like my repousse triangular solid earrings with the scroll motifs, because the scrolls are not the same on the two earrings.

A pair of earrings affords a dimension that little else can about the wearer. When Clara Schumann went to Paris in 1832 and gave a piano concert at age thirteen, she was presented as a lady, not a child prodigy. Her stepmother dispatched a Frenchwoman to go shopping with her so she would perform dressed a la mode. What better to make Clara look grown up than big gold dangles? Clara's stepmother's brother sketched her portrait — heart-shaped face, wistful large dark eyes, and hair drawn from a middle part into a high chignon. She wears a scarf over her off-the-shoulder gown, and the torpedoes that suspend from her rather pointed, back-slanted ears are quintessential for the Romantic period: textured gold bodies and stylized tops, yet modest at just under two inches, not overpowering her face or youth.

France: Marie-Amélie

Marie-Amélie (1782–1866) lived a fraught yet un-tragic life that brings the old regime to a fairly quiet conclusion. Her mother was queen of Naples when Marie Antoinette, the mother's sister, was queen of France. The two sisters decided to betroth their children, so Marie-Amélie was raised to be a royal, as was Louis-Philippe, son of the Duc d'Orléans. French revolutionaries beheaded the French queen, ending a royal match. Although the Duc d'Orléans favored a constitutional monarchy, he was forced into exile in Switzerland with his son, Louis-Philippe, who had to beg lodgings until he found a job teaching mathematics at a Swiss private school. When the Directory released Louis Philippe's two younger brothers from a Marseilles prison, part of the deal was that they and Louis Philippe, a Bourbon pretender, sail to America. The brothers traveled to Cuba and around the United States; in 1800, they settled in England.

In the meantime, Marie-Amélie was evicted from Naples when Napoleon invaded in 1789. Horatio Nelson, the British naval hero, helped Marie-Amélie and her family escape to Palermo. In 1809, Louis-Philippe traveled from England to Palermo to thank the king, Marie-Amélie's father, for having offered refuge to his brother. There, he met Marie-Amélie. She was twenty-seven, intelligent, refined and, what's more, a Bourbon. In her journal, Marie-Amélie wrote: "I have made an acquaintance which will probably influence my whole life, and has given rise to new sentiments and ideas in my mind and head." They fell in love and married. When Napoleon fell from power, Louis-Philippe and Marie-Amélie were once again royals-in-waiting. Charles X abdicated in 1830, and the French legislature chose Louis-Philippe as king and Marie-Amélie as queen.

Known as the "citizen king" or "bourgeois monarch," Louis-Philippe eschewed luxury. Marie-Amélie bore ten children, and they were a home-loving couple, so home-

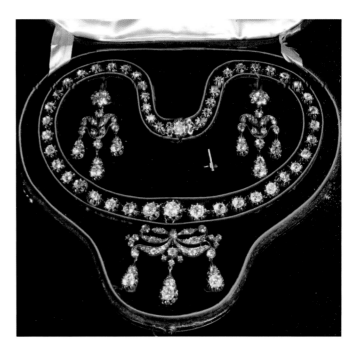

English girandole (1830).
Source: Hancocks of London.

Gold and banded agates.
Source: Brenda Ginton.

Etched and cannetille.
Source: Jane Merrill.

Jean-Baptiste Regnault,
Hortense de Beauharnais.
Source: Giraudon Bridgeman Art Library.

loving that many French people — with short memories — faulted the royal couple as lacking in regal stature. (It is said Louis-Philippe had a pretend mistress for state occasions to satisfy the expectations of the populace regarding royal lifestyle.) Their reign ended with the Revolution of 1848, and concluded gracefully with a last exile to England, their heads still intact, where they won the friendship of Queen Victoria.

I see in Marie-Amélie a modest queen and good mother, very dignified, yet dressing prettily. She occasionally wore plumed, beribboned rather grandiose bonnets. The parure she chose to wear on the rare occasion she needed to dress to the hilt was her personal possession, not from the French crown jewels, which she never touched. It has a piquant history. The parure was created from fine diamonds and Ceylon sapphires, once Hortense de Beauharnais's property, inherited from her mother Josephine. However, the earrings were apparently unchanged and are, after two centuries, in the original condition, having survived the 1880s Republican dispersal of royal jewelry.

Day-night.

Louis-Philippe was scrupulous about keeping his monarchy to a modest scale. Like all nineteenth-century kings of Europe, he took his lesson from the fate of Louis XVI. From his personal funds, he commissioned Evrard and Frédéric Bapst, popular jewelers to Europe's royalty, to redesign it for his queen. The pendeloque earrings feature pearls, diamonds, and sapphires, with gold scroll and leaf work fitting with the rest of the parure. A layer of diamonds tightly clusters around a small emerald in the top element and an immense one in the lower element. The earrings, visible in a portrait of the bejeweled and plumed lady, are exceptionally royal, like costumes for the theater, and beautiful as well. Their eclectic style derives from neo-Classical and neo-Gothic, which makes them archetypal for the Romantic times.

Ironically, this is the only complete parure in today's collection of French crown jewels. For much of the state's jewel collection was sold off under the Third Republic in the 1880s. The earrings are on permanent exhibition in the Apollo Gallery at the Louvre.

Source: The Colonial Williamsburg Foundation.

Vermont Lady

Hanging in the Colonial Williamsburg collection, the *Lady with Gold Earrings* (1835–1840) is a Vermonter. She wears a low-cut black dress with leg of mutton sleeves, severe like her pulled back hair, making her one adornment all the more striking. I find the earring that is visible in the portrait and how she wears it mesmerizing. It is composed of a gold wire that supports a lozenge suspended from one corner. A long gold drop hangs below the lozenge. Expressively, the earrings follow the languorous geometry of her body. Like a small gold plumb line the long drop underscores the sitter's gravity or rectitude. Yet this gleam of gold is central, the sole spot of ornament amidst the severe play of black hair and dress, and white flesh. The artist, Aaron Dean Fletcher, painted the portrait in Springfield, Vermont, when he was about twenty, before a long career as itinerant painter. His somewhat naïve artistry has caused the perpendicular drop earring to stand out compositionally as the one vertical amidst the play of curves (neckline hair comb and jawline). It tries to pull your eye left, away from the woman's compelling gaze. It also creates, with the curve of her ear, and the arc of the comb, a partial secondary frame for her face. In fact, it might also read as a soft inverted exclamation point.

Diamonds owned by Elizabeth Taylor (1830).
Source: John Bigelow Taylor.

plot device that silently expresses the mindset of one woman, the dairymaid Hettie, and reveals her to another, Hettie's cousin, Diana, a Methodist lay preacher. From a linen press, she takes an old black scarf and, from a secret drawer, a pair of large earrings. Hettie lights the stubs of candles and admires herself with a hand mirror she otherwise keeps hidden. "And she would take out the little ear-rings she had in her ears — oh, how her aunt had scolded her for having her ears bored! — and put in those large ones: they were but coloured (sic) glass and gilding, but if you didn't know what they were made of, they looked just as well as what the ladies wore."

Looking dreamily at her own image, drawing her hair back from her face, and donning the fine earrings and lace fichu, Hettie feels sure the squire's son will "want to marry her and make a lady of her." Soon Diana awakens and Hettie drops the mirror, and reaches for her Bible with alarm. The earrings had a seductive power. Yes, Hettie is vain and wants to be beautiful for somebody else, but her self-absorption is more natural and normal. She struggles not with vanity, but with the social order. Decked out in jewelry, she hopes to recreate herself, to leave her social place, and meet her heart-throb as an equal.

Hands.
Source: Nadine Karkov Collection.

Hands (other side).
Source: Nadine Karkov Collection.

Coach covers.
Source: Glorious Antique Jewelry.

The 1860s and '70s, with their fanciful and faithful motifs on pendant earrings, enchant me. Dresses took on bows, braid, pleats and ruffles, and draped overskirts, and they merited longer, more elaborate earrings with highly decorated surfaces. Even headstones and shell cameos might be dressed up with earrings and neck-laces of tiny stones. Fossilization, to borrow a term from costume historians, also occurred where the upper-class wore what Marie Antoinette or du Barry might have, deliberately preferring old-fashioned designs, like girandoles, to stand up for the regime. Predictably, in reaction, earrings would become neat and small from about 1880.

Franz Winterhalter, *Portrait of Empress Eugenie*.
Source: Chateau de Compiegne, Oise, France, Bridgeman Art Archive.

Eugénie

Historically, ambitious women, movers who married or slept their way to fortunes or lofty ranks, hopped into luxury's lap, and by and large possessed the most extravagant jewelry. During the French Second Empire (1852–1870), courtiers strove to keep their place in the musical chairs of a new empire and spent lavishly on earrings and necklaces. Cartier's was founded at this time. Eugénie, empress to Napoleon III, impulsive, energetic, and athletic, developed into an iconic fashionista. Her father was a Spanish grandee of republican persuasion who fought in Napoleon Bonaparte's army and remained loyal to Napoleon until the last gasp. Her maternal grandfather was a Scotsman whom George Washington appointed counsel in Malaga, Spain.

In her mid-twenties, Eugénie was still single because her first love rebuffed her in favor of her sister. Eugénie tried to kill herself by drinking poison, so her mother removed her from the scene of disappointment and took her around Europe, with the usual objective. Eugénie glimpsed Louis-Napoleon in 1836 when he passed through Paris. Despite slim odds, mother and daughter pursued him. When Eugénie caught up to and formally met the august prospect, he had failed to overthrow the restored Bourbons by a rash attempted coup from exile, but he had imperial prospects all the same.

Eugénie built a life on her philosophy of being the consort of a great man. Indoctrinated with the Napoleonic cult by her father and her mother's friend, the novelist Stendhal, she learned the prince's modern program of governing from his own book, *Des Idées Napoléoniennes* (1839), where he argued for Bonapartism as the optimal way to replace aristocracy with meritocracy and democracy in France. Louis-Napoleon invited Eugénie and her mother (along with a hundred guests) to Fontainebleau and then to Compiegne, the rural palace where the Bourbons had hunted. He was twenty years older than Eugénie, and might have been expected to marry European royalty, but he fell in love and wrote a statement to the people of France how she represented the breath of fresh air the new empire needed. A week after he proposed, they married at the Tuileries and Notre-Dame (civil and religious ceremonies).

Various cities offered gifts, and Paris voted to give Eugénie a diamond necklace, which she turned down, asking for money for a training school for poor girls instead; the school was built in the form of a necklace, a semi-circle of buildings, in her honor. In the bridal basket, Louis-Napoleon gave her the same necklace.

In response to the plain living of the Citizen King, Louis-Philippe, Eugénie embraced her responsibility to restore more than a touch of luxury. Her husband encouraged her to wear fancy clothes and jewels in order to stimulate the luxury trade (laces from Alecon and Valenciennes, silk and velvet from Lyon, and so forth). Together, they recreated the court of Napoleon I. Whereas Louis-Philippe forbade his wife from wearing the old regime's jewelry, Eugénie regaled in it. Most of the pre-1789 pieces had disappeared, but she wore the pear-shaped earrings of Marie Antoinette. She also had many jewels reset.

The empress was a pacesetter. She popularized crinolines, invisible hairnets, colored petticoats, and summer umbrellas — rather practical fashions, even the crinolines being easier to ambulate in than some previous skirts. Eugénie surpassed in opulence princesses at the other courts of Europe and Russian, yet the designs of the elite cadre of jewelers, like Chaumet, were graceful and fine. She liked jewelry best in a naturalistic style, like flowers, ivy, and currant leaves.

Long pendants can be found in the antique shops of Europe because Eugénie wore them and they became the prevalent style in the 1860s and '70s for dress-up. They weren't always set in precious stones. Dante Gabriel Rossetti portrayed Monna Vanna in 1866 (a painting at the Tate in London) as a pre-Raphaelite goddess. She wears a rich garment with Ottoman design, several long amber bead necklaces, nautilus hair ornaments, and prominent, red gold earrings, with a stylized big daisy suspended from a smaller flower.

Charles Worth, an Englishman who, as an expatriate in Paris, became the world's most famous couturier, kept one showroom, the Salon de Lumiere, dark as night. Mirrors lined the walls, and gas jets had movable shades so the lady could see herself in her ball gown as she would be seen the next night at the Tuileries. In the context of Worth's showroom, jewelry shone like pebbles at the beach when wet.

In France, jewelry designers kept fashion abreast with politics. Ladies in the know were partial to *vert Bonaparte*, *rose reine Hortense* (after the Emperor's mother), and *bleu Elysées*. Later came two new colors — Crimean green and Sebastopol blue — that called for splashy effects on one's ears. Eugénie also revived the lilac blue that Marie Antoinette had liked, and the number one color of society in 1863 became Maximilian, another blue shade, due to France's military adventures in Mexico.

Eugenie's love story didn't pan out, however: Louis-Napoleon was promiscuous in the tradition of his uncle. A staircase from his study led to a bedroom above where a pretty lady who had caught his attention would wait in the buff. If he didn't fancy her, he would say, "I am summoned by my papers," and she was led out. He grew rheumatic while the younger Eugénie loved to ice-skate on ponds and parks in Paris and swim in the Atlantic Ocean. Their only child died in the Boer War. After her husband was ousted from power in 1870, she passed her last years in the English countryside.

Conscious of her duty, Eugénie wrote in her memoirs: "The public judge by externals and thought I was only interested in smart parties and fashion, dresses and jewellery (sic). I was blamed for being frivolous... If only they could see my notebooks." She sponsored *lycees* for women and gave to many charities. Thus, during the Second Empire, her husband allowed her 1.2 million francs per year, of which 100,000 went for clothes and most of the rest for presents, pensions, and charities. Yet she was fond of her jewelry and saw the empress in the looking-glass. If she wasn't as heavily made up as Marie Antoinette, she used rice powder on her skin and kohl on her eyes, and rouged her earlobes! Curiously, being fanciful as well as generous, she had jewels reset in the garland style of Marie Antoinette.

In 1855, Louis-Napoleon and Eugénie sailed from Calais, going on a state visit to England. They boarded a fast mail steamer while another boat carried Eugénie's hairdresser, wardrobe, and jewel boxes. A heavy fog delayed the second vessel. When she arrived, the Empress had no jewels or hairdresser, and was due to dine at Windsor Castle with Queen Victoria. One of Eugénie's ladies lent her a blue silk dress, and they put a nosegay of forget-me-nots in her hair to replace the jewels. At the state banquet, her simplicity captivated the guests. When the French regents bid adieu to Victoria, the emperor reopened the carriage door, jumped out, and threw his arms around Victoria and kissed her on both cheeks.

George Cruickshank, *Ladies ears bored.*
Source: Courtesy of The Lewis Walpole Library,
Yale University.

Frederick Sandys, *Grace Rose.*
Source: Yale Museum of British Art.
Paul Mellon Fund.

Victoria

Queen Victoria (1819-1901) liked to wear color and heavy fabrics as a young woman. She wore flowers in her up-do, and long earrings, almost to her shoulders, in the Romantic style. Etiquette held that earrings were not to be worn by young girls, so it was a special coming-of-age present when King William gave her diamond earrings for her fourteenth birthday. (Victoria would give several daughters diamond earrings at sixteen.) She influenced women to dress in a solid homey fashion, but the bright dresses and hoop-skirts encouraged long or substantial earrings.

In 1838, Thomas Sully, the American painter, did a famous portrait of Victoria at nineteen in full coronation regalia, including long, top-and-drop pearls. What the queen bought and wore is carefully recorded in a royal ledger by Garrard, her favorite jeweler. She considered diamonds regal and, except during her most profound years of mourning, wore them. The diamonds were usually brilliant-cut; she had emeralds from the Empire and her favorite rubies. Elizabeth II wore diamond earrings on her coronation day that were made for Queen Victoria, using diamonds from a ceremonial sword and a ruby from a treasure of the Lahore maharaja, which the East India Company gave her.

Saccharine might describe some of the mourning jewelry of the era, for which Victoria set the style (it was required at the English court 1861-1880), but art historians are taking a new, more sympathetic look at this jewelry of sentiment. The impulse was not to display the wearer's feelings, but to console her. Nevertheless, wearing jewelry of a deceased's hair could take on tones of the macabre, something Robert Browning exploits in his poem *The Laboratory* (1842), one of whose stanzas associates earrings with the dead and dying. Here the speaker exults to the apothecary that his poison can go into the smallest receptacle belonging to the woman she hates: "Had I but all of them, thee and thy treasures,/

What a wild crowd of invisible pleasures! To carry pure death in an earring, a casket,/ A signet, a fan-mount, a filigree-basket!"

Albert adorned Victoria with personal jewelry that was different from the tiaras, necklaces, and garters of state. Because she loved flowers, he gave her a parure of life-like orange blossoms of white porcelain. Two blossoms, one in bud and one opened, dangle from the frosted gold leaves with green enamel oranges on the wreath for their four children. Albert grew up in Thuringia, where it was a custom to mount stag teeth into jewelry. In England, he hunted stag and had dainty earrings, now in the royal collection, with leaves of gold made for her from stag horns. Victoria herself had earrings made out of her children's milk teeth.

Queen Victoria kept her jewelers busy resetting jewelry. In 1858, she commissioned a diamond necklace and earrings that have the collet (raised collar) setting from an old badge of the Garter order. The necklace included the Lahore Diamond, which weighs nearly twenty-three carats, and has twenty-nine diamonds, adding up to a weight of over 160 carats. The earrings followed the typical design of large diamonds on top and smaller ones below, with large pear-shaped drops. The Queen had a pair of large matched brilliant-cut diamonds set as studs.

In Victorian times, a middle-class family likely had a silver tea service. It could be plate once the electroplating was well established. If there is a trying situation in a British drama set in this period, or later, someone offers a spot of tea. The etching on the silver resembles the patterns of scrollwork, curving lines, and geometry on studs and dangling Victorian earrings. Similarly, those ubiquitous pieces of Victorian silverware — the epergne and teacake stand — look like giant earrings. Mechanized jewelry-making by the latter part of the century made jewelry affordable to the expanding middle-class. Finer earrings were either handmade or a combination of machine-made parts and handcraft, as they are today.

Fringed drops.
Source: Brenda Ginton.

Pique tortoiseshell.
Source: Glorious
Antique Jewelry.

Memento.
Source: Exceptional
Vintage

Hair jewelry
(Civil War period).
Source: Mur-Sadies
Estate Jewelry.

Whimsy

We go to the 1860s and '70s for the splendid variety of earrings, large and small, revivalist and realist, for evening and day, with the unusual motifs and *en tremblant* flowers, and night-evoking deep blue enamel and balls and carved shapes of polished jet. Earrings were central to a fashionable look. "In jewelry a locket and ear-rings are sufficient for a set," said an 1869 fashion piece in *Godey's Lady's Book and Magazine.*

Earrings were a chance to show the jeweler's skill and, like lucky charms, there was everything from little coffee pots and cannons to wear to the races, to clusters of amethyst grapes and gold-rimmed beetles or real hummingbird heads implanted with gold beaks. The Victoria & Albert museum notation on a pair of hummingbird earrings notes that Harry Emanuel, who took over his father's London jewelry business in 1855, elaborated the work in ivory by adding feathers and plumage. This technique made Emanuel rich and earned him a post as a diplomat.

Just as archaeological revival jewelry could show that a woman had made the Grand Tour, whimsical earrings could be an assertion of a woman's special interest: she wore croquet mallets because she was good at the game. They could also refer to being a "Mrs." to a man's identity, such as his cycling or his being a

Lily Martin Spencer, *Kiss Me and You'll Kiss the 'Lasses* (1856).
Source: Brooklyn Museum of Art.
A. Augustus Healy Fund.

naval officer. We can't know if they were worn with a wink, jolly humor, or boastfully. There is one painting that proves the novelty earrings could have a sexy or flirtatious subtext, *Kiss Me and You'll Kiss the 'Lasses,* by the popular painter of domestic American scenes, Lilly Martin Spencer. She looks out, brandishing a big spoon of molasses (the "lasses") as if to smack a man who grabs and kisses her. Yet she wears tiny basket earrings, repeating the motif of the harvest fruits providing her with work. By this time, those who saw a reproduction of the painting in their magazine knew of or had played "A-tisket a-tasket/A green and yellow basket/ I wrote a letter to my love/ And on the way I dropped it," that most erotic of circle games, which, in the adult version, someone outside the circle drops the handkerchief behind somebody else, and is chased and, if caught, kissed. The pictured woman with basket earrings pauses to turn to flirt, and, since the earrings look authentic, not stagey, they might have been a real pair that the artist depicted.

Coral jewelry was popular among Victorians for its color and elaborate carving. Coral earrings took the form of fruits, flowers, vegetables, cherubs, hands, and faces. The flowers all had special meanings — the language of flowers was a subject of countless pretty little books. For instance, the most popular floral motif of the day, the forget-me-not, stood for steadfast love.

Coral cameos.
Source: Antique Rarest Cameos.

Micromosaic.
Source: David Frith Jewellery.

Stone cameo locket brooch and earrings.
Source: HW Antiques.

Repousse silver flies.
Source: Suzy Lemay,
Watford, United Kingdom.

ENTER CHARLES DARWIN

In 1859, Darwin made public his theory of evolution in O*n the Origin of Species*. Unfazed by how it contradicted with creationism, jewelers in England and on the Continent borrowed, often with an intense accuracy, from the kind of flora, fauna, and geology that Darwin reported from many lands during his voyage on the HMS *Beagle*. Darwin inspired earrings using motifs of insects, bees, monkeys, and invertebrates, as well as the peacock feather, Darwin's key to understanding courtship and mate selection. Frog earrings sat in realistic bulrushes. There were earrings made of fossils enclosed as jade or onyx might be in silver. Fly earrings were popular because flies are attracted to the sweetness and the execution was pure entomology.

In the 1860s, the vogue for insects was brisk. Earrings arrested the movement of the insects yet wearing the earrings re-animated them. They also idealized nature, such as a nest of bird's eggs not in peril of snakes or raccoons, but set in aesthetic perpetuity. In his *Curious Relations* (1866), William d'Arfey gives this description: "Bonnets and veils were covered with every kind of beetle; that at least was the beginning of the mode, but it soon extended itself from rose-beetles with their bronze and green carapaces to stag beetles...Parasols were liberally sprinkled with ticks, with grasshoppers, with woodlice. Veils were sown with earwigs, with cockchafers, with hornets. Tulle scarves and veilings sometimes had on them artificial bed bugs..." These insects when they appeared on earrings were often finely wrought and certainly eye-catching.

Hummingbirds.
Source: Museum of Fine Arts, Boston. Museum
Purchase with Funds donated anonymously and
by Joanne A. Herman, Susan B. Kaplan and Textile
Curator's Fund.

Bohemian garnets.
Source: Jean Papin.

AN IMPRESSIONIST FOND OF EARRINGS

Critics used to fault the Impressionist paintings as too pretty; however, they depicted the world around them, and this was a very pretty time for fashion. When the founding group of artists exhibited in 1874 constituted a high time for earrings, and of interest is how the two most prominent women of the movement did with their sketchy brushstrokes about earrings. All of us who like jewelry should pay tribute to Berthe Morisot (1841–95), a very honored Impressionist who in her portraits of friends and family repeatedly focused on their garb. It's frustrating to scrute these complex, fashionable earrings for information on what the ladies actually wore. In each case, the earrings seem representational, but on second look they aren't. We see the earrings, we blink, and poof, they were just strokes of color and light. It was the same when she posed for Edouard Manet: we see jet Maltese crosses, or do we?

Berthe came from an enlightened *haut monde* family that let her and her sister Esme follow the career of artist. She exhibited with the "rejected" painters and became a friend, perhaps lover, with Manet, posing for him, encouraging him to paint outdoors, and marrying his brother Eugene. The sisters painted each other with earrings. In Esme's picture of her sister at the easel (1863), Berthe looks beautiful in action, wearing work clothes and archaelogical revival earrings.

Berthe put no earrings on the mother in the often-reproduced picture *The Cradle*, but when her portraits show women dressed or dressing up for a luncheon, theater, or a ball, they wear distinctly styled earrings and often a ribbon necklace. The earrings vary from gold pendants to long black fringed drops to pairs where quick strokes of unblended paint reflect and become lost in the color of a background, or, in *Madame Boussier and Her Daughter* at the Brooklyn Museum of Art, a purplish velvet gown.

By contrast to Morisot, Mary Cassatt (1844–1924), from Pittsburgh must have thought earrings a bit uncon-

Turquoise enamel.
Source: Jane Merrill.

ventional, because her portraits did without. In several paintings, Cassatt articulated a subject in reverie by having her idly touch her unadorned ear. The exception is one of only two known self-portraits, done in 1878, the year after Edgar Degas invited her to exhibit with the Impressionists (a show delayed until 1879). In this gouache on paper, now in the Metropolitan Museum, the artist, asymmetrically posed, wears a hat with a big sash that does not disguise one long, gold drop, whose diamond-shaped pendant suspends from a wide horizontal surmount, and which brings out the red-gold strands in her hair.

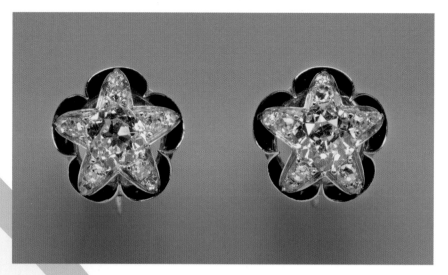

Wedding gift to Elizabeth Colt (1856).
Museum purchase with the Frank B. Bemis
Fund, William Francis Warden Fund, and
funds donated anonymously.
Source: Museum of Fine Arts, Boston.

Enamel and pearl cherubs.
Source: The Three Graces.

Classic drops.
Source: Rau Antiques.

Gold and coral.
Source: Brenda Ginton.

Puzzle knot.
Source: Artisans Antiques.

Victorian fashion drawing.
Source: Jennifer Thomson.

Etruscan revival.
Source: Lang Antiques &
Estate Jewelry.

Etruscan revival.
Source: Rau Antiques.

Marriage set: seed pearls
and horsehair.
Source: Brenda Ginton.

ON FIFTH AVENUE

In the 1950s, Fifth Avenue was one big candy box
of jewelers, from Harry Winston and Tiffany to Bulgari and Swarovski. I was curious to see the Victorian
naturalistic motifs and what seemed like examples of a
charm bracelet period for earrings: exquisiteness and
whimsy combined. A La Vieille Russie, the legendary
antique jewelry store, had gold flower baskets and other
pairs they kindly agreed to show me. The jeweler had
described horseshoe, housefly, and bumblebee motifs,
as well as something like goldfish in a bowl and parrots
in a cage — a pair circa 1865–1870 of bird's nest-motif
earrings. I expected whimsy-like hanging plants. Instead
these were miniature sculptures. A dainty and kinetic
pair had little white enamel birds on perches. I admired
them and then the jeweler brought out the bird's nests.
These were magnificent, as superior to just cute earrings
as a Benvenuto Cellini cup is to a gravy boat.

Nests of pearl eggs.
Source: The Three Graces.

Multicolor cluster.
Source: The Three Graces.

Pink and green gold.
Source: Newark Museum.

Jouaillier box.
Source: Rau Antiques.

THE ACTIVE WOMAN

This was the time when women were beginning to enter the public sphere. They put on their earrings and not just discreet little buttons, but individualistic choices and whimsical ones, too. They were "sportive." Walt Whitman wrote of these women: "They know how to swim, row, wrestle, shoot, run, strike,/ retreat, advance, resist, defend themselves,/ They are ultimate in their own right – they are calm, clear, well possess'd of themselves." I like to think of Sarah Orne Jewett equally at ease going out in a boat for sport in the Penobscot Bay or playing a mean game of croquet or horseback riding up into the Camden hills as wearing her finery in Boston or London.

Sporting earrings had dangling charms or the picture worked into a design. These tended to be silver or silver gilt. There were crossed oars, symbols of archery and rowing, roulette wheels, croquet hoops with crossed mallets, tennis rackets or a hand holding a racket and ball. The newer sports were most represented: the four-wheeled indoor rollerskate in the late 1860s and the bicycle in the 1880s.

A kind of portrait, or *habillé*, cameo showed a fine lady "dressed up" in jewelry, like a necklace and earrings, with a little diamond. The tilt of a nose can indicate a more recent portrait cameo whereas the old-fashioned ones had "Roman" noses. Two small bacchante in the set of peach salmon cameos of Sardinian coral have masterfully carved faces. This material became fashionable just after the marriage of the Duchesse d'Aumale and a Prince of the Two Sicilies, who presented his bride with some exquisite coral ornaments in her *corbeille*, in 1845. It remained very popular until 1865. George Augustus Sala, writing in 1867 when the vogue had somewhat declined, noted that a few years before, people had gone about "bedizened with twisted sticks of seeming red sealing-wax. Their coral earrings had an unpleasant resemblance to fragments of ginger or orris-root, or even the domestic forked radish smeared with red ochre." The coral he describes was worn in its natural,

is the type of jewelry that encapsulates a past and thus has nostalgia built in." For earrings cameos are perfect because an antique mask in agate, coral or chalcedony could be set in a frame like a portrait.

Tiffany's was continuously linked with high-profile clients, such as the American socialites who created a stir with their marriages to foreign nobility. As early as 1859, a sketch of an heiress's pendant diamonds, part of her bridal jewelry, appeared in a New York newspaper. In 1856, Sam Colt, inventor of the revolver, bought for his wife, Elizabeth, a suite in which repeating fat diamond flowers are enclosed by black enamel. Abraham Lincoln gave Mary Todd Lincoln a seed pearl set costing $530, which she wore to the inauguration. After their son Willie died in 1862, she went on a shopping spree. This, according to Boston Museum of Fine Arts Chief Curator Yvonne Markowitz, is probably when she bought a demi-parure from a Washington, D.C. jeweler — with earrings of cushion (mine) cut diamonds prong-set in silver, with the jewels outlined in black enamel tracery like the eyes of a Siberian husky. She had to sell these beautiful pieces to pay the bills when she was widowed. The earrings originally had ear wires, but were refitted with screw backs. A black onyx set with diamonds that she allowed herself to be photographed in publicly may have served as mourning jewelry.

Mid-Victorian mass production centers included Providence, Rhode Island, Newark, New Jersey, and Birmingham, England. In slang, the latter was mockingly called "Brummagen" because some of the machine-made trinkets were poor quality. On display at the Providence jewelry museum are actual dies used for earrings produced in specific weeks and months. In New Jersey alone, Newark was gold, silver, and leather, Paterson was silk, and Trenton was pottery and porcelain on a par with Staffordshire. The first American factory for manufacturing fine jewelry dates from 1801, in Newark.

Louis Hersent, *Marie-Amelie de Sicile*.
Source: RMN-Grand Palais, Art Resource, New York.

Lady Wearing Spectacles (c. 1840). Gift of Edgar William and Bernice Chrysler Garbisch.
Source: National Gallery of Art, Washington, DC.

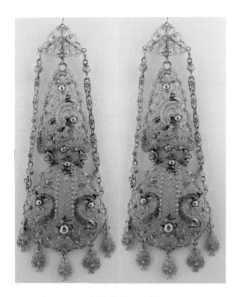

Filigree, probably from the Netherlands.
Source: Adin Fine Antique Jewellery

Acorn day-night.
Source Brenda Ginton

Diamonds and sapphires.
Source: Lang Antiques & Estate Jewelry

Gold-wrapped garnets.
Source: The Three Graces

Reprise

A book reproducing the treasures found in excavating Nineveh, Layard's *Nineveh and its Remains*, came out in 1848 and jewelers made bracelets and earrings based on Assyrian patterns. This was the beginning of the Archaeological Revival that marched through the nineteenth century. With most of the Victorian jewelry reworking historic motifs, antiquarian jewelers give high marks to the Castellani brothers, who, in Rome and Naples, capitalized on the wave of archaeological discoveries in their times to work in the archaic style. When they reproduced Neo-Classical jewelry, they mastered the ancient techniques, especially granulation and filigree, instead of just imitating the forms. The Castellanis studied the techniques used in the ancient jewelry that was being dug up in Etruscan tombs, and were the great archaeologists of the world of art. They presented Napoleon III with their work, which became famous at the 1867 Paris Exhibition and soon was displayed by jewelers the world-over. In the movie *Gone with the Wind*, when Rhett Butler (Clark Gable) marries Scarlett O'Hara (Vivien Leigh), he gives her luxuries that she had been deprived of during the Civil War, among them archaeological style of earrings.

Eliza Johnson, the wife of Andrew Johnson, the first president to come into office after the Civil War, also followed the trend. She posed wearing Archaeological Revival long earrings in a portrait photograph. She and the president were poor folk from Raleigh, North Carolina (his mother was widowed of a shoemaker), and they married at sixteen and nineteen. She taught him arithmetic, and helped him advance in reading and composition, so finery must have had significance for her. The next First Lady was the opposite: Julia Grant grew up with a personal preference for emeralds, sapphires, and rubies, and is photographed, since earrings were shrinking during Grant's tenure as president, with single drops.

Neo-Gothic motifs are endemic and frequent. Where the furnishings of the Gothic Revival reach some comical excesses, the jewelry tends to be more modest. The decorative motifs on cathedrals employed include the crossed curves at the top of windows (tracery) and quatrefoils, as well as interior decorative motifs of pelleting (beads without holes) and tassels. Rarely is a Christian cross a pendant or motif and earrings were too dainty and feminine for great piety, so the Gothic Revival earrings are lovely. How the style came about shows the vagaries of design. A French draughtsman expatriate to England taught his son to draw. The son, Augustus Pugin, grew up with French influence and eventually converted to Catholicism. He designed buildings, including the clock tower known as Big Ben, and the interior of Westminster Abbey, as well as stained glass, metalwork, textiles, furniture, and jewelry. In 1852, he died young of exhaustion and his sons carried on the firm to continuing influence.

While the neo-Gothic architectural movement was launched in architecture in the 1740s, it wasn't until the third quarter of the nineteenth century that looks like buttresses and arches were widespread in jewelry. The Queen relaxed her mourning rules in the year of the Golden Jubilee (1887) and diamonds were discovered in South Africa in 1867. Electricity was installed in many public halls throughout England in about 1880 and the jewelry became lighter and brighter with more colored jewels. Tiffany's, for instance, which ruled high-end jewelry trade from its beginning in the 1850s, was using Australian opals, blue sapphires from Montana, and pink tourmalines from Maine. Tapered drops imitated the lines of foliage.

We love Victorian earrings above all not for the gemstones or even the superlative workmanship, but because they seem to speak sentiment. The giving, receiving, and wearing of them all belonged to a mystique between men and women. Honore de Balzac wrote the *Physiology of Love* to try in that self-improving age to establish a template that would improve romantic relationships. Women liked love tokens, but if one couldn't afford good jewelry what was a poor young man to do? Balzac declared the opinion that "to know how to offer the ear-rings in such a way that they will be returned is a secret whose application embraces the slightest details of life."

This brings me to my single, favorite pair of Victorian earrings, where whimsy is executed with perfect craftsmanship, resulting in utterly wearable fantasy. You see this pair of goldfish bowls that were a *tour de force* in rock crystal. If you've carried a goldfish in a bowl or plastic sack back from a country fair or amusement park, you know that the bowl sloshes and almost tips out the fish. The same giddy tension was embodied in these earrings. Some earrings had a sense of humor, with a mouse traveling on the gold of a hoop, or on a candlestick nibbling a candle. The costlier ones would have sapphire and ruby eyes, but a woman without the wherewithal for these could have fun silver ones made in Birmingham, or Providence, Rhode Island.

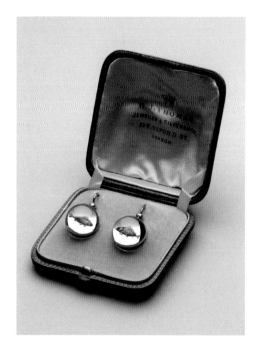

Goldfish in bowls (1870). Source: Trustees of the British Museum.

Newark: Earrings for Every Woman

Ulysses Grant Dietz, *Senior Curator, Newark Museum*

Between the 1850s and the 1950s, Newark, New Jersey, probably produced more women's earrings in 14k and 18k than any city on earth. I'm not making this up. With roots in the early 1800s, Newark was, by the time of the United States Centennial in 1876, the undisputed fine jewelry capital of the nation, with scores of factories, workshops and studios ranging in size from half a dozen workers to five hundred. Millions of pieces of gold jewelry for men and women emerged from these varied shops and were sold, quite literally, by every retail jewelry store in America, from Miami to Nome.

The reason this was so was that Newark produced fine jewelry for the vast American middle class market. Beginning with the tariff of 1842, American jewelers could compete more and more easily with foreign imports, and the influx of skilled German jewelers from cities like Pforzheim, because of European unrest in the 1840s, encouraged this trend. At the same time, the same industrialization that made jewelry production more cost effective produced a thriving consumer economy and a prosperous middle class that wanted all of the trappings of aristocracy — at a price they could afford. Newark itself became known for the guaranteed quality of its jewelry. Most of the women who wore jewelry made in Newark never knew they were doing so: the name on the jewelry box was always local, and always a retailer. Newark was famous only in the trade; but within the trade its name was, literally and figuratively, as good as gold.

The year was 1872, and an immigrant Newark manufacturing jeweler named Ferdinand Herpers patented the very first prong setting for showcasing diamonds in the Western hemisphere. The patent is for an asterisk-shaped setting with six notched prongs. These were intended specifically for the new flood of high-quality diamonds coming from the Kimberly pipe in South Africa, the first great new source of diamonds since Portuguese discoveries in Brazil in 1729. Herpers arrived in Newark in the 1840s and worked as a bench worker for two decades before opening his own shop in 1865. Herpers was the first American jeweler to focus on the production by machine of findings for the jewelry industry, as well as in producing finished jewelry for the wholesale market.1

The Newark museum owns a pair of pendant earrings using the Herpers patent setting which descended in the family and were given to the Museum in 1937. In 14k rose gold with hinged ear wires, they are assembled from multiple small parts made in the Herpers shop, and reflect the dominant Renaissance or neo-Grec style of the decade immediately after the Civil War. The earrings are decorated with black enamel and set with glass stones – the only reason they made it to the twentieth century. They are an extremely rare survival of this period, since real diamonds would long since have been recycled into more modern settings. For all their structural simplicity, the stones intended for these earrings (which have a matching brooch) would have made them very costly. Tiffany & Co. would certainly have sold earrings like this, purchased without stones from Newark manufacturers, to showcase their own diamonds.

Also in Newark's collection is a pair of earrings with a coordinated brooch, also by Ferdinand Herpers, that represent typical 14k middle class demi-parures of the 1880s. These three-part sets were a staple of the prosperous middle-class market in fine gold jewelry all across the nation. Ornamented only with small seed pearls and some added hand-engraving, they represented the most elaborate solid-gold jewelry available at the least cost at the time — offering a housewife the most bang for the buck. These three pieces, clearly intended for retail sale as a boxed set, were probably assembled as a sample, since the colors of the gold aren't entirely consistent. Although they would readily enough fit into the generalized "Islamic" or "Arabic" style that appeared in the decorative arts in the 1880s, a close study of the three pieces makes it clear that they were designed to take advantage of a multiplicity of small mass-produced parts that could be put together in a number of ways. Herpers sold this wide range of findings to allow other regional manufacturers in cities all across the nation to design and produce their own jewelry using pre-made parts.

Of course, earrings continued to change stylistically as fashion dictated; but it wasn't only the style that changed. The most important change in middle-class earrings is reflected in this pair from the turn of the twentieth century by Newark's largest manufacturer, Krementz & Co. George Krementz was the son of an immigrant Indiana farmer, who moved east and joined the throng of Germans working in Newark's burgeoning jewelry trade. He opened his Newark factory in 1866, a year after Ferdinand Herpers. Unlike Herpers, the Krementz operation produced a combination of high-end production jewelry and mass-produced accessories, like the man's collar button. By the turn of the twentieth century, Krementz was the largest single manufacturing operation in Newark.2

What makes these earrings distinctive are two elements: the use of enameling, for which Newark became famous from the late 1890s onward; and the use of screw backs, a type of earring that first appears in the 1890s and continues to dominate the middle-class market until the late 1930s. The short art-nouveau-inspired form of water lilies set with small opals reflects changing taste at the end of the 19th century. The screw backs reflect something else entirely. Piercing the earlobe had been the standard mode of fastening earrings since ancient Egypt. However, by the early twentieth century the pierced ear had become problematic for middle- and upper-class Americans, because of its association with the huge influx of poor Eastern and Southern European immigrants into the nation's cities from the 1880s on. A custom that had been expected for millionaires' wives in the 1880s had become much less acceptable for their granddaughters in the 1910s. The pierced ear would not regain dominance until the 1960s.

So these exquisite little art nouveau sculptures are modern in form, in style, and in technology. They reflect the dominant trend for middle-class fine earrings up until the moment when the clip-back changed the geography of the earring landscape yet again in the 1930s.

The final pair of earrings for consideration is also part of a suite: a pair of pink gold roses with green gold leaves made by Krementz to go with a necklace of the same combination. These bear the Krementz maker's mark (a collar button in profile) as well as the retail mark of Tiffany & Co., and are important documents to the fact that the highest-end retail jewelers in America continued to rely on Newark's manufacturers for their less expensive lines well past World War II.

Earrings like this, worn ensuite with a matching necklace or brooch, would have been seen as appropriate for daytime wear with the tailored suits of the late 1940s and earl 1950s. The simple, bold design was part of the aesthetic shift in the 1940s toward stylized floral designs that relied on different colors of gold for their visual impact. Although clip backs had been introduced in the 1930s, screw-back earrings continued to be used, although their popularity would wane rapidly in the 1950s, especially as the scale of earrings grew larger, making the screw-back impractical to use.

Particularly interesting is that this suite very closely resembled the rolled-gold (i.e., plated) rose blossom jewelry for which Krementz was becoming famous under its own brand name at the same period.3 Although the introduction of rolled-gold jewelry in the 1930s kept Krementz healthy during the Depression — which saw the collapse of many Newark jewelry manufacturers — they never ceased making fine jewelry as well, which was invariably sold without the brand name to retailers in the great tradition of Newark jewelry making.

While the big-name jewelry retailers such as Tiffany and Cartier in New York, Caldwell and Bailey in Philadelphia, Peacock and Spaulding in Chicago, and Shreve in San Francisco, produced their own high-end jewels for their wealthiest customers, they always turned to Newark manufacturers for their less elaborate "bread-and-butter" jewelry. These earrings would have been that type of jewelry, and Tiffany's most likely would have required exclusive use of this design for sale under their name. Retailers such as Tiffany typically did not want the maker's mark on the pieces they retailed, but enough double-marked examples surface to suggest that it was not uncommon. The general public had no idea what the makers' marks were and only recognized the retailer's name.

[1] See Dietz, Ulysses Grant, Jenna Weissman Joselit, Kevin J. Smead, and Janet Zapata, *The Glitter & the Gold: Fashioning America's Jewelry.* Newark: The Newark Museum, 1997, pp. 17, 42, 171.

[2] Ibid, pp. 173-175.

[3] Ibid, p. 127.

The Belle Époque: Bows and Bouquets

" *The way to love anything is to realize that it might be lost.* "

~ G.K. Chesterton

Gold with rose cut diamonds and green tourmaline (1890-1900). Source: Brenda Ginton

Gold with diamonds (circa 1900). Source: Brenda Ginton

*E*arrings faded out like the old salt print photograph during the late Victorian era. Long matte gold etched or niello gold drops, pendants of coral or lapis lazuli, and my beloved novelty earrings dissolve before our eyes as we look at the fashion plates in the last quarter of the nineteenth century. Now roundness dominated ears, and the more vertical pairs were dainty and fine. Their scrolling filigree, threaded drops, and miniscule tassels, bows, ribbons, and flowers are called, because of their being strung together, the garland style. The ladies parading in the plates of *Godey's Lady's Book* had elaborate hairstyles, and hats in all seasons, indoors and out. Their earrings were pearls in tassels or just little dangly, diamond solitaires in silver settings (*dormeuses*), and rose-cut diamonds surrounding pastel stones or pearls. You could still buy girandoles at Tiffany's (now with a showroom in Paris), but the big change in the new century came with the array of more modest earrings sold at the jewelry counters of B. Altman's in New York, Au Bonheur des Dames in Paris, or the new Marshall Field in Chicago.

Edwardian Grandmothers

The Edwardian Era is magical to me because this was when my adored grandmothers were girls. The grandmothers, tall, slender Edwardian schoolteachers from well to do backgrounds, lived proudly on very reduced means as single women most of their adult lives. They were, I heard it said, opposites, but in their excellent character, and making do, they were alike. Emma told me about her and her sister's beau rowing them to the old mill for picnics: from a painting by my grand-aunt, I could visualize them in long white dresses, straw hats, and high-top shoes. Once, on the way home, the horse took fright, and the carriage overturned, and... Alice, my father's mother, talked about riding horses and traveling with her mother, an opera singer, and all the fun on Peak's Island (Maine) before she got polio in about 1902.

Platinum and diamonds. Source: A La Vieille Russie

Moonstone.
Source: Three Graces

Silver pendants
with gold
fasteners.
Source: Adin Fine
Antique Jewellery

Red coral drops.
Source: Adin Fine Antique Jewellery

What valuables Emma had were heirlooms. From a farm, musical and bookish, a retiring widow, she had jewelry of gold and lovely stones, mostly gifts in her youth (she was born in 1888) from family. When she became elderly most pieces were as old as she was. She dressed in printed lawn cotton dresses in summer and dark silks in winter, and besides wearing her jewelry let me have it to incorporate into my play. She had a fancy belt and shoe buckles, a fine locket with diamonds on a chain, and, as people once said, sets of "good pearls," but I liked best the floating opal necklace suspended from a matte gold cone, and its matching opal earrings like tiny flowers, with the same scrollwork on their gold leaves. She owned several pairs of rose-gold and pearl, screw-back pendants, probably not worn to the Methodist church, and different designs of round enamel and silver earrings, more arts & crafts than art nouveau. I played that the cobalt blue pair melting to cream, with iridescent red centers, were supernatural eyes. Emma prized above the other earrings a pair designed with two round white diamonds of graduated size. My grandfather had them made for her from stones on the fobs of his pocket watch.

My other grandmother, Alice, coming from the barely populated Maine island, loved big cities and luxury. When her children grew up, she left my grandfather (the doctor who treated her polio, older by 25 years). From then until age 80, concealing her true age, she supported herself as personal assistant and companion to the wealthy, e.g., Amelia Earhart's sister in New York, or living in Harriet Beecher Stowe's house in Litchfield, Connecticut. Alice shopped at department stores like Jordan Marsh in Boston and Saks & Company in New York, and coordinated her jewelry to the colors and style of her dress. She shopped at Tiffany's and kept the volume of her total possessions to two large suitcases. This had to be why she liked earrings so much — they were small.

I admired her old earrings like the marcasite silver screw-backs of a flowery pattern, with the little cushion to hold them on, which came from her youth, but Alice preferred bright clip-on enamel earrings by, possibly, Schlumberger. She used to tell me that her gold dollar pieces, some made into a set of jewelry (I picture only the dollar-charm bracelet), and some loose coins in her jewel box were more valuable than her Tiffany diamond ring, which I could not understand. Jenny Lind gave these to Alice's mother when Alice's mother traveled with her during Lind's American tour. Presumably, both my grandmothers, like most middle-class girls at the turn of century, would have considered piercing uncivilized.

In *An American Tragedy*, Theodore Dreiser described a pretty turn-of-century girl's diminutive earbobs:

> *A small scarlet bow of velvet ribbon at her throat, two small garnet earrings in her ears, a very trim and tight-fitting black dress, with a heavily flounced skirt, seemed to indicate that she was not opposed to showing her figure, and prized it, a mood which except for a demure and rather retiring poise which she affected would most certainly have excited comment in such a place as this.*

Diamond drops.
Source: Lang Antique &
Estate Jewelry.

Cameos (1910).
Source: Richard W. Bell

Art deco onyx and diamonds.
Source: Soho Jewelers

At the same time, overall jewelry was turning into art. Jewelers combined mythic and folkloric subjects with Renaissance or biomorphic designs. The tendrily ornamentation lasted twenty years and came to an end at the beginning of World War I. Asymmetry and naturalistic curves associated with art nouveau figured little, however, in earring design. Art Nouveau looked great on metro entrances, posters, and furniture, but women's ears called for balance and more recessive beauty. It stretches credulity that anybody wore, for instance, the designs we see of art nouveau fantasy earrings. For example, Paris jewelers Fanniere Freres matched with a brooch of goddesses and Neptune a pair of earrings with prong-set large diamonds at the ear, from which suspended mermaids with snaky hair. Their torsos jetted forward, and tails spiraled back in contra pose, the scales on their elongated forms dripping with pearls.

Jane Stanford

The garland style — the inordinately delicate fili-gree, white on white, and raised milgrain beaded edges that look like embroidery — may not have major visual impact, but they seem like the most gentle of earring styles. These refined, feminine earrings clearly matched in lightness and pallor the dresses, and so I imagine one day discarding my conventional wardrobe to become an elegant old lady who dresses in white and plays lots of croquet and lawn tennis. I note that I have a few pairs of earrings with lacy openwork and decorated ear hooks to "gild" the look, the vision of which appears more than literally getting old and wearing purple. Mind you, *belle époque* earrings were elective accessories and the lacy ones were for the rich as Midas.

A famous woman who did like to have herself photographed in earrings was Jane Stanford, wife of Leland Stanford, attorney, railroad magnate, and gover-nor of California. For three years at the outset of their marriage, the Stanfords were separated. Leland went to California to make his fortune with his brothers while Jane took care of her father in Albany, New York. In her mid-20s, Jane felt ostracized by people who may have thought her husband had abandoned her. She made up for this palpably by eventually having perhaps the biggest, single jewelry collection of her time, described as second only to the British and Russian crown jewels. Jane proudly wore earrings and her jewelry had a fasci-nating and significant history.

When their fortunes soared, Leland lavished jewelry on his wife, including various items once belonging to Empress Eugenie of France and Queen Isabella of Spain.

In Europe, they snapped up diamond parures, principal-ly of yellow, brown, pink, blue, and white tints, but also purchased a pin and a pair of earrings of oblong opals set round with diamonds that had a provenance that had put off other prospective buyers.

The opals were milky blue with an uncommon fiery red spot in the heart of each stone. The jewels had been in the possession of an unmitigated series of very unfor-tunate persons: Hungarian nobility, then a lady in wait-ing of the Empress of Austria, from her new husband who soon died; then a Spanish family in duress, that pawned them to Empress Eugenie, whose aid they had received. It was said Eugenie only wore them once due to the misfortune that had come to all previous owners. However, the doleful stories did not deter the Stanfords, who had already suffered the great loss of their only son; they acquired the opals in 1886, from a Genoese jeweler at the Centennial Exhibition in Philadelphia.

In 1893, when Leland Stanford died, the university the Stanfords had founded in memory of their son was in trouble, as the assets of Leland's will were frozen. Ap-parently, to give to charity, Jane went to London to sell her jewelry collection during Queen Victoria's diamond jubilee. People were distracted and the economy was be-low par, but Jane auctioned off the jewelry, which is why she had Ashley David Cooper paint a still-life study of it before the sale. The collection's earrings (the painting is in the Cantor Arts Center in Palo Alto) display Gilded Age elegance, featuring *en tremblant*, filigree borders, airy rococo touches, and the lacy openwork which make earrings seem akin to brooches. Jane left another fortune in jewelry to Stanford in her will, for the express purpose of a fund for books at the university library.

D.M. Astley, Jane Stanford's jewelry.
Source: Stanford University Archives

Icing the Aristocrats

Diamonds set garland-style in platinum, say with pearls and slightly rococo, can seem gaudy — but just right scaled down as earrings — the way a detail of a vast narrative painting may be more pleasing to view than the whole. I admire the earrings on Princess Alice, born Alice Heine in the U.S.A., who reigned over Monaco from 1889 to her divorce from Prince Albert in 1902. The model for the Princess of Luxembourg in Marcel Proust's *A la recherche du temps perdu* (translated into English as *In Remembrance of Things Past*), she chose to wear pearl earrings with her extravagant six-strand pearl chokers bound together by diamond bars. When Clementine married Winston Churchill in the fall of 1908, she wore diamond earrings, but she also wore amethysts and peridots, and we can imagine her a large, bright dragonfly flitting around the Churchills' garden parties.

Black opal and diamond,
American (circa 1910).
Source: A La Vielle Russie.

Enamel with gold
screw backs.
Source: Newark Museum

Micromosaic
butterflies.
Source: A La Vielle
Russie

Jade, diamond and enamel,
English (circa 1905).
Source: A La Vielle Russie.

Platinum

It's the purest, hardest, haughtiest, and rarest of all precious metals used in jewelry. More subtle in its lustrous whiteness than silver, and far less flashy than gold, platinum evokes both the candlelit wit of a formal evening and the mirror-like cool of a modern skyscraper. Its aloofness holds a mystery, a quality less of glowing sentiment than of serene authority, which has long made it the preferred setting for a spirited diamond. Platinum is actually the world's "noblest" metal, a term which, chemically speaking, means that it will not tarnish, like silver or steel, turn green like copper, or crust like aluminum. Indeed, short of a bolt of lightning, platinum, like Cleopatra, is sublimely indifferent to the corrosion of time and atmosphere.

From 1900 platinum became the metal of choice for famous jewelers such as Faberge and Cartier. It was strong and durable and bespoke drop-dead elegance.

Ever adaptable, platinum became the rage of the Art Deco period; its sleekness of surface suited the strict mood of the times. Zelda Fitzgerald cherished a platinum and diamond watch, which she turned over and over to read the inscription, "From Scott to Zelda," on the back. Scott Joplin's platinum watch caught the stage light as he rolled out his ragtime, and Cole Porter's wife, Linda, presented him with a whole collection of cigarette cases, one for every show opening, many of them platinum. Mary Pickford picked platinum earrings to wear with her pearls; Jean Harlow was platinum, and Greta Garbo, of the regal reserve, understandably preferred it. So established was the elegant ascendancy of platinum that no less an arbiter than the Duchess of Windsor proclaimed: "A fool would know that with tweeds or other daytime clothes one wears platinum."

Although most of the world's supply of gold has a leisurely nonexistence in the underground vaults of nations, platinum is a metal that goes to work — and then out to dinner. Heavier than gold, it is more useful and rarer — a fact little suspected by the Spanish conquistadors, who found it mixed with the gold they panned in South America. They dubbed it "platina," or "lesser silver," and tossed it back in the river as worthless stuff. Today, most of the world's supply comes from a 20-inch subterranean lode known as the Merensky Reef in South Africa and from the eastern slopes of the Ural Mountains in Russia. Its scarcity is hardly surprising as it takes eight tons of ore to produce one ounce of metal, five times the proportion for gold.

Platinum alloyed with ruthenium or iridium — both members of the platinum family of metals — has long been the diamond's best friend. The color of sparkling platinum provides a perfect setting because the metal is self-effacing, luring attention to the diamonds rather than to the mountings. Pink, yellow and blue sapphires, canary and white diamonds, amethysts, tourmalines, and aquamarines are the colored gems jewelers claim hold up best to platinum's uncompromising flash. In an interview in 1983 Claude Arpels, president and owner of Van Cleef & Arpels said, "Sapphires are aloof stones and their coolness suggests intellectualism and deep-running passions. They match and reflect the same quality in platinum. Rubies and aquamarines look right with platinum too, so long as their color is rich."

In the Art Deco period, Van Cleef & Arpels evolved the "invisible setting," which made other jewelers sigh with envy. Due to a ribbed backing of platinum wire, a field of gemstones seemed to float unattached to the setting.

The only time Van Cleef & Arpels did not work in platinum was during the Second World War, when the metal was restricted for war use; it was needed for the manufacture of gunpowder. "The poster said 'Platinum is going to war'," recalled Mr. Arpels. "It was unpatriotic to sell it. We substituted white gold or palladium, but they both have a slight grayish tinge, and jewelry from that period is definitely inferior."

In the experimental 1980s, a fashion trend was to use platinum in combination with other metals, particularly 18-karat gold, and Paloma Picasso designed for Tiffany's matching bracelets, earrings and necklaces of latticework platinum; at every juncture in the lattice, she placed a tiny barrel set with a diamond, the grid evoking forms at the molecular level.

Platinum's association with stylistic innovation and the spirit of modernism got its greatest boost in the Twenties. The master jewelers of the period — Louis Cartier, Raymond Templier and Boucheron — made platinum supreme. Its icy, lean look represented a conscious rejection of Victorian stuffiness; further, Jazz Age wealth was new wealth, and wanted the metal with the drop dead elegance. Comments Patricia Suling, jewelry expert and former manager of Fred Leighton, the Art Deco emporium in New York, "The mood and temper of the Twenties was a complete break with the past, and platinum was a break with established metals."

Diamonds were only part of the era's earrings story. Women at the top of the social scale and also middle-class favored earrings with cabochon-cut gems that reflected a silky "chatoyancy," the luminous line running across the fibers of the gem. Moonstone, beryl, cat's eye, tiger's eye, tourmaline, and opal all have it. For example, Cartier made a pair of earrings with tiger's eyes from banded brown quartz in 1883. I thought the "broken rainbow" hues of my grandmother's floating opal like nothing else in the world, although she assured me that many of her friends wore moonstones and opals. Iridescence has an eternal appeal.

European and American aristocrats came to their full power after dark; thus jewelry was made to dazzle in artificial light. Evenings on the S.S. *Titanic*, women put on their valuables, wearing earrings with long gowns and capes or fur stoles. Helen Cristaux, widow of a Montreal businessman and philanthropist, took her children on a vacation to Europe and booked one of the *Titanic's* expensive suites. Her jewelry case held sparkle aplenty including earrings with pink oval diamonds surmounted by white diamonds.

La Belle Otero's Earring Trick

Actresses and courtesans had an unprecedented influence on chic in this period. I'll begin this explanation with a personal story:

My American family moved to Paris in the late 1950s. Thanks to a prostitute we met while walking our dog, we moved out of the impossibly expensive George V into a small hotel on Avenue la Boetie, near the Étoile. With Jeanette, we dined across the street at a five-table restaurant, where a vacuum cleaner hose had been rigged up as a fan. While my father worked, my mother, brother, and I went with Jeanette to parks. We took tinned

meat, baguette, and thermoses, and played cards and catch. She talked about being a working girl as my mother hushed my brother and me out of earshot. We sprawled long afternoons in the "bois" on a blanket with books borrowed from the American Library, and soon my fifteen-year-old big brother had permission to take me out around the Étoile on our own. We both had pocket money since we did small services for the hotel manager and bartender. Tom saved his for the stamp market while I bought antique postcards. When it rained hard and the wind swept down the café chairs in front of the hotel, we crossed the Seine to the stalls along the quais, where many *bouquinistes* stayed open, jacking up their little awnings. The images that mesmerized me were old photographs, some tinted, of somnambulists, coquettes, and dancers of bygone days, posed like Renoir's women, but spicier because the women often wore lacy lingerie and black stockings and had a come hither look that I used to try out myself in the mirror. The most familiar model had dark hair and a defiant look that epitomized farouche. I liked her, and because she appeared in so many different outfits, from evening gowns to the frilly dress of a Spanish dancer, I could imagine her as a real person and imitate her dance. The postcard *femme fatale* was identified as "la Otero."

Caroline Otero (1868–1965) embodied the razzle-dazzle of entertainment. Among the demimondaines who tweaked the rules of nineteenth century society she had the most brazen reputation. The papers tallied her high-profile swains and receipts of deeds and jewels. She came from Galicia. Her mother had four sons and two daughters, and no husband. She bought castanets for the daughter who was a vivid dancer as a child. One day, as she walked in the woods, the village shoemaker raped and nearly murdered the girl. After that, the vil-

William-Adolphe Bouguereau,
Boucles d'Oreille (1891).
Source: Private Collection, Bridgeman Art Library.

lagers shunned her. She recalled in her memoirs a sweet existence that when she was eleven went up in flames. Six months later, she took the name of her dead sister, Caroline, and, with the help of impresarios who would also be among her lovers, she made her way in the world singing and dancing. Her performances in Barcelona, Paris, and New York were filled with fury and energy, like an exorcism of her childhood trauma. She wrote in her memoir that childhood troubles "penetrate deepest… their hurt is most complete and hopeless."

In 1890, at age twenty-one, la Otero made her American debut at the Eden Musée, a combined wax museum and performance hall at 55 West 23rd Street, in front of a posh crowd. A reporter who inventoried the crowd remarked on Mrs. Whitney Belmont's tiara and "the solitaire earrings, weighing 30 carats each hanging modestly from the lobes of Mrs. Frank Leslie's ears." The exotic Spanish dancer created a sensation in New York and became a media goddess. She made up stories that her father was a general and marquise, and newspapers followed her every move, gourmandizing on how she spent the nights with clients who besieged her and the jewelry they gave her. The American playboy, William Kissam Vanderbilt, newly divorced, crossed the Atlantic in his yacht and fetched for Caroline the matched pearls Louis-Napoleon had once given Eugenie. Over the next six or seven years, he gave her a large Tiffany collection. A French biographer said the belle epoque was a schizophrenic society "ever torn between the values of respectability and the vertigo of unknown pleasures."

Caroline took her act all the way to Russia, where her offstage life included being served naked on a tray to a table of guests of a wealthy host. Among her lovers were Prince Albert of Monaco, King Leopold II of Belgium, Prince Nicholas I of Montenegro, Grand Duke Nikolai of Russia, and the Prince of Wales, before he succeeded Queen Victoria as King Edward VII. She referred publicly to their relative virility and vaunted her sexual encounters like sports matches. Vague about her

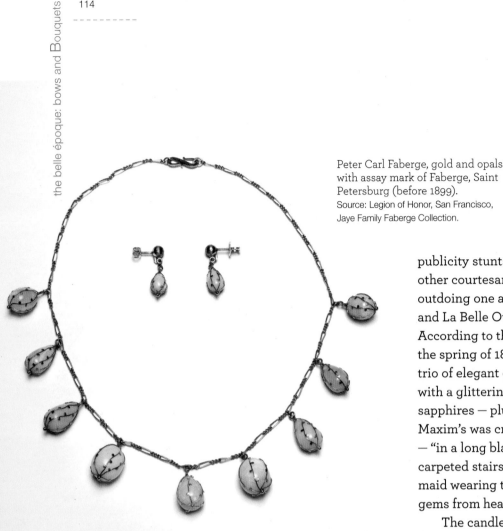

Peter Carl Faberge, gold and opals
with assay mark of Faberge, Saint
Petersburg (before 1899).
Source: Legion of Honor, San Francisco,
Jaye Family Faberge Collection.

publicity stunts among the demimondaines. Liane and other courtesans of the period gathered at Maxim's, outdoing one another with their baubles from admirers, and La Belle Otero and Liane de Pougy fought publicly. According to the *New York Journal*, late one evening in the spring of 1896, Liane entered Maxim's squired by a trio of elegant gentlemen, bedecked from head to foot with a glittering array of jewels — pearls, emeralds, and sapphires — plus a diamond tiara. The next night, when Maxim's was crowded, Caroline made her own entrance — "in a long black simple gown she swept up the red-carpeted stairs jewel-less. But behind her was her house-maid wearing the dress de Pougy had worn, loaded with gems from head to toe."

The candle of a courtesan burned brightly, but soon flickered out. Liane married a Romanian prince. When he divorced her for his secretary, Liane joined an order of nuns. After the First World War, Liane saw Caroline on the Champs-Elysées, still with a beautiful face, wrapped in furs and huge pearls in her ears, bearing herself proudly, but she was fat. Yet Liane esteemed her rival. When a journalist compared Caroline to another actress, Liane interrupted him: "See here, sir, when Cavalieri wears real jewels they appear false, but when Otero wears fakes they look completely authentic." Prey to her gambling addiction, Caroline died in poverty — a disappointment to those who flocked to the auction of her possessions where they found only trinkets, for her life at the casinos had consumed the rest.

Partly from many, many moves and partly by nature, I'm not good at keeping things. This is why my daughter, Rosalind, an English graduate student at Princeton, is the "family archivist." One April, I came home from a trip to find a flood churning in the basement of my farmhouse. Since the house had only two flattish closets, I'd had the cellar fitted out for storage, and dancing on the surface of my basement floor, along with my passport, were the belle époque ladies, some of whose cards I dried out and saved.

life, she had total recall of her jewel collection and could reel off, chapter and verse, the gifts men so willingly bestowed on her.

When a tour to Italy was a failure, solace came back in Paris from a Prussian, Baron Ollstreder, whom she had thrown over at Longchamp earlier that year. On the nights he wanted her, he sent on ahead a box from Cartier with a jewel and his calling card, but one night at the opera he left her for a few minutes to talk with a countess. Caroline tore off one of her earrings (a gift from the baron) and left in a huff for a café where they often had a late supper. The baron came after her and found her fuming. "When you have the honor of being with the Belle Otero," she said, "no one else exists." Blamed for the loss of her earring, Baron Ollstreder promised her a new pair. Meanwhile, the earring was safe in Caroline's bodice. Calming down, she told the baron he could give her a magnificent diamond necklace for reparation, which he did.

At the Folies Bergère, Liane de Pougy was famous for an act where she wore a diamond pasty on each nipple. Dining at restaurants was a new phenomenon for women in the nineteenth century, and it encouraged

Literary Allusions

European tourists to Asia, as in E.M. Foster's novel *A Passage to India*, dreamed of glamorous new experiences. Earrings in this time period witnessed a high point of Indian influence because many British traveled to India. This led to tutti frutti jewelry, the multicolored arrangement of gems, which makes such striking earrings. At Cartier's, the designer Jean Toussaint, who favored the Mughal exotic look for herself, made jewelry of carved emeralds, rubies and sapphires with little diamonds tucked in. The Pasha of Egypt wore Cartier cat earrings. Naturalistic forms evoked flowers in the garden of a Persian potentate.

The Alexandria Quartet by Lawrence Durrell, set in Cairo in the late 1930s, was high on the list of cool novels we read when I was in college. To me the *Quartet* was like a magic lantern into "the Orient." It played a part, like E.M. Forster's *A Passage to India*, in propelling many of us to travel far abroad. The narrator says, "The gold *cigales* [grasshoppers] of Justine's ears transformed her at once into a projection from one of his dreams and indeed he saw them both dressed vaguely in robes carved heavily of moonlight." A grasshopper plays music, is feminine and, in La Fontaine's fable, both carefree and careless. Durrell was playing with literary French tradition, although it's conceivable that the Justine character wore earrings with insect motifs. Elsa Schiaparelli, for instance, used rhodoid plastic for jewelry in her "pagan collection" (inspired by Botticelli) in 1938, where colorful, toy-like metal insects were trapped inside the clear plastic. The insects might have been in prehistoric amber except for all their pretty hues, and also surreally looked as though they were crawling on the wearer's skin.

Only in the Art Deco period did an important opera's story hinge on earrings. In 1925, Viennese audiences first heard the musical theme "Marie's Earrings" in Alban Berg's avant garde *Woyzeck*, based on the

Theater Magazine (Jan. 1924).
Source: Bridgeman Art Library.

Set Mysteriously

The white on white, flowery designs of Edwardian jewelry segued into streamlined geometry in design. Thus it was in this epoch that the invisible setting was invented, a prime example of the love affair that designers had with technology. Taking advantage of straight edges, in 1933 Van Cleef & Arpels launched the invisible setting, which has been their specialty ever since. Gems are placed side-by-side, and grooved, with hidden metal wires laced underneath. This holds gemstones aloft for sleek Art Deco cascades and unbroken fields of gemstone color. According to Nicolas Luchsinger, Director of Van Cleef & Arpel's Heritage Division, historically the setting descends from micro-mosaics and represents the tightest of pavé: "Instead of hard stones we went to precious stones, and you absolutely do not see how they are set. Creation of these ribbons of light takes extreme coordination between the stonecutter and the jewelry maker and is very time-consuming. It is rare to recognize a jewelry house by their work, but such is the case with the Serti Mystérieux, which became a signature technology of the Maison to present day." He adds, "It is a very fashionable and recognizable technique. Wherever you go, everyone knows you are wearing Van Cleef."

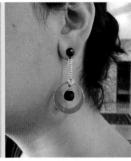

White gold set with diamonds, onyx, pearl and chalcedony.
Source: Brenda Ginton.

incomplete play of the same name by Georg Buchner. I was unprepared for the opera when I was invited to it in Munich. As so often with operas, the females come to a tragic end, but the scenes in this opera pop out of nowhere like nightmarish visions, and the five-note fragment "Marie's Earrings" reappears until it becomes recognizable (like motifs in *Peter and the Wolf*). Watching the anti-hero go berserk and murder his mistress, who accepted a gift of earrings and sexual favors from a drum major, is an experience of unredeemed pathos — that the opera was based on a real crime story from the century before, of a wigmaker who killed his lover in a jealous fit, adds to the wretchedness, while the little earrings theme is innocent and Ophelia-like. The earrings were ill gotten and Woyzeck kills Marie for taking pleasure in them.

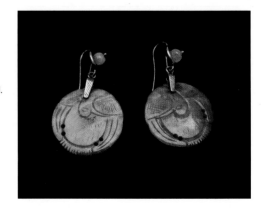

Jade discs.
Source: Jane Merrill.

The primitive look was fashionable for sophisticated Europeans and, in Mexican religious folk art, e.g., ex-votos painted to work a miraculous cure, even the Virgin Mary wears earrings like girandoles. However, Frida mixed elements to amazing effect in her paintings, and created her masks and her image that is as unforgettable as an artist. As her health declined — a traffic accident left her crippled as a child — her jewels and flowers became more colorful. Masking her pain, she showed herself to the world as a festive figure like a bright piñata.

Frida had great success with other painters. In 1938, she had her first international exhibition in Paris. She stayed with the surrealist, Andre Breton, then with Marcel Duchamp's girlfriend. The exhibition was a *succes d'estime* and the great artists she met — Joan Miro, Yves Tanguy and Max Ernst — admired her work. Kandinsky lifted her up in the exhibition room and kissed her as tears ran down his cheeks. Picasso regaled her with compliments and gave her a pair of earrings. These had a surreal touch. They were tortoiseshell hands with gold cuffs. Picasso taught her a Spanish song, "The Orphan," that had the line, "I have neither mother nor father to suffer my pain. I am an orphan." Later she would sing this to Diego and friends in Mexico.

Floral dangles.
Source: RomanovRussia.

The Providence Jewelry Museum

The Jewelry Museum that Peter Dicristofaro founded and directs tracks the jewelry industry through time. When the industry of the jewelry quarter of Providence, Rhode Island, was being destroyed in the 1980s, as cheap jewelry was coming in from Hong Kong, he bought the original molds, artifacts, and gadgets. Hundreds of drawers are intact so Peter says, "the man at the bench is preserved — it's like Tutankhamen's tomb."

The early industry in Providence made coin silver spoons. All over Colonial America the ovals of spoons were the same. If nested into the Providence spoon they would fit perfectly because they were formed in a die press. Then came the cladding of a metal of more value over one of less value, like silver on copper, a process that began in England.

Dicristofaro points to an anthology of styles and techniques:

"We have the whole Linton factory (1854–1985) when it went out of business. We bought everything. The small company had international clientele for hatpins to watches. The maker of costume jeweler was free to make what he wished, unlike the fine jewelry, which did costly items with stones, and was curtained in by what he could buy. The hubs, soft steel dies that are hardened, show the history of all manufactured jewelry in America. They are hand cut and in themselves original steel sculptures and often masterpieces of working in metal. From them came the basis for jewelry for Tiffany's and Sears's. The die doesn't lie; 120 years later we can make a piece of jewelry with it. We can pinpoint a style of earrings to the very week it was made and marketed.

Mid-20th Century: Over the Top

Dressing up the ears, whether gypsy-style for Jane Russell, lustrous Hobe for Ava Gardner or archaeological revival for Vivian Leigh playing Scarlett O'Hara, characterized glamour prior to and in the wake of World War II. Sometimes studios decked movie stars out like Christmas trees. Barbara Stanwyck, playing a bedridden hypochondriac in *Sorry, Wrong Number* (1948), sits up in bed wearing a lavish set of figural diamond and platinum jewelry from a new shop on Rodeo Drive in Beverly Hills. However, there really were two looks — daytime and gala, unassuming versus big and bold.

Audrey Hepburn, pictured more often in daytime clothes, was a minimalist — "Put me in furs and jewels and I look like something off a barrel organ." She was most herself in simple diamond and pearl buttons. Grace Kelly too was a model of subtlety with earrings as discreet as if she were already a princess. Most middle-class housewives wore earrings and gloves when they left the house to go downtown — the delicate earring and necklace sets of a Betty Draper on *Mad Men* — just part of the prescribed uniform. But when they dressed up, women followed what they saw on the screen, or in the glossy magazine (not just more rich ladies, as status had in fashion begun to level out), and became sparklers.

The leitmotif was being ladylike but as glossy as your lipstick. It was not a youth culture, and being a grown-up meant conforming to a standard of good taste. Thus, when movie star Loretta Young hosted a television show and, around 1960, overdid the mascara and blindingly sparkly diamond studs — they shot icicles of light from her dainty ears — viewers in my house laughed. Loretta should wear aurora borealis clusters, pearlescent starfish, sprays of citrine, or porcelain flowers. Oh dear, one of my elders might remark: "Was this what the girl-next-door did if she could?"

Rita Hayworth's sapphire-ruby-diamond-studded favorite earrings ended up adorning the world's most expensive shoes. Stuart Weitzman nestled the clips on the rust-colored satin ruffles of the toe boxes of a pair

Diamond and platinum waterfall.
Source: Lang Antique & Estate Jewelry.

Pink globes by Miriam Haskell.
Source: Brenda's Treasures.

Honey-colored cluster
by Miriam Haskell.
Source: Brenda's Treasures.

Oak leaves by
Miriam Haskell.
Source: Patricia
Hanten.

of d'Orsay pumps. Varying the tradition of redesigning jewels, mutatis mutandis, the designer adapted but did not break down the earrings. Actress Kathleen Bird York wore the Rita Hayworth Heels to the 2006 Oscars; now they belong to Rita Hayworth's daughter, Princess Yasmin Aga Khan.

My personal taste doesn't incline to mid-century jewelry. Growing up, my friends and I put the fashionable earrings of this period in a category with circle pins — not cool. They signified submitting to old roles. However, while looking at jewelry on my path for this book, I was struck by what a sophisticated antiques collector told me: "It doesn't have to be your personal taste. Look with an unblemished eye; some is so outlandish but you might see it as an art form." Viewed with this understanding, the earrings of this period draw us in as jewelry's festive period. Christie's and Sotheby's auction some costume pairs by Kenneth Lane as though they were precious gems (and they looked lovely and appropriate on several First Ladies), and designers like Miriam Haskell, "Juliana" and Trifari today still evoke Ali Baba's cave of excitement: handmade beads, fine metalwork, and overall gorgeousness.

Tiffany starburst.
Source: Lang Antique &
Estate Jewelry.

Juliana: Tracing the Marks of a Mid-century Jeweler

Bob Brown, *Aged and Opulent Jewelry*
Based on his Juliana, DeLizza & Elster Jewelry Education Site, www.julianajewlry.net

For forty years William De Lizzi and Harold Elster produced costume jewelry for many companies. At first the rhinestones were handset. In 1967, they began using the trademark "Juliana" on paper tags (no name was ever incised on the jewelry). Juliana is characterized by multilayered, multicolored stones of different sizes and spectacular design.

When looking at "Juliana style" earrings by Delizza & Elster, first you check for the figure 8's. You ask what are figure 8's?...two round settings that are joined with solder that look like a figure 8. Then you look at the backs and see if you can find excess solder, and you continue looking at the back and see if you can see any castings (casting are metal poured into mold to create a shape). At one point in time, Delizza & Elster used the wire over method, which was when a piece of wire was soldered on the back and bent over to the front, and more settings were added at the end to create more dimension. Then you check the clip of the earring. The most common one used had a single hole in it but later they had three holes in them. There have been examples of screw back earrings but are harder to find.

Delizza & Elster made the earrings in style with the times. Some were plain and then you have the very elaborate combinations of settings and stones. Some of these design traits are clustered or cascading (dangles), and would complement other pieces of jewelry in the suite. A major part of Delizza & Elster aka Juliana was the stones they used. They used every cut — navettes, marquis, oval, round, emerald-cut, baguettes — and they also had fancy shapes or cuts, that is, Rivoli, marguerita, keystones, triangle, diamond, kite, and fan. Some of the most popular have the pointy-topped Rivoli's and for color heliotrope stones (also called watermelon). It is a thrill to find the beauties today because they don't make them anymore with the stones and the rhodium plated settings. These earrings were made to last the tests of time and the designs are timeless. The women who wore this jewelry have cherished these pieces and have been known to pass them down to their daughters. So keep your eyes open for these beauties.

Before the flashy, busy shades and textures of gold in the '50s, women adorned their ears with the flaring colors and jaunty, curvy designs of the '40s, of which Sylvie Raulet writes in Jewelry of the 1940s and 1950s, "Every jeweler without exception explored these bold juxtapositions, creating symphonies of original colours which made these somber years seem less austere." What looks at first blink like earrings may be dress clips to offset the square neckline of dresses, and plainness of suit jacket lapels. Mid-century engraved metal has patterns extending even on one piece from engraved lines to fluting, stippling, piercing, and coiling.

Jewelry had political purpose in the Second World War. In 1942, a gold and enamel brooch called "Bird in a Cage" appeared in Cartier's window on the Rue de la Paix. The little bird had outstretched ruby wings and tail feathers. The Gestapo summoned Jeanne Toussaint, Cartier's artistic director, to the Hotel Majestic where she answered defiantly that she had always liked birds, and was using a design that preceded the war. When Paris was liberated, Cartier celebrated it with a "Bird at a Door of its Cage" with coral breast and lapis wings, looking as though it would burst into song. Other Parisian jewelers feted with their creations as well: Mellerio did tank brooches, Mauboussin fighter planes, and another Paris jeweler designed earrings with parachutes.

After the war, women wore costume jewelry — rhinestones, silver or gilt braids, shell motifs, and dangling elements. Schiaparelli's double clips had a cluster on top of the ear and another at the lobe. Women were buying a lot of jewelry for themselves, without a care, and having fun with it, which explains the profusion of animals, like a Cartier bracelet ending in panther heads that could be taken apart and worn as earrings.

Hairdresser styling
the hair of Marilyn
Monroe (1950s).
Source: The Image
Works, New York.

A Mother's Jewelry Box

Many of us can return to our grandmother's or our mother's jewel box. What I see in my mind's eye is from the 1950s, when my mother's femininity fascinated me. Eye-catching necklaces went with the earrings. She wore jewelry to jazz up the dark suits and bowed white silk blouses she wore as a Jersey girl modeling in New York City and as hostess at Delmonico's where she had to look elegant on a single woman's modest income. My mother wore no sets; she considered that old-fashioned. Her jewelry items had big and dramatic forms like seashells, starbursts, and ribbons, in yellow or rose gold, with rhinestones or tiny diamonds inlaid in broad gold surfaces. She wore half-spherical pearls, called *mabe* and kid leather earrings fashioned to look just like orchids, lilies, and rosebuds. With a brown Harris Tweed suit she wore a pair made of feathers that looked like peahens.

Whether screw-ons or clip backs, either way they made her ears sore, and she took them off with relief after the occasion. She did not wear earrings at home, not even when she dressed for dinner, but a suit, cocktail dress, or flowery sundress to go out merited earrings.

Pearl-tipped florals
by Kenneth Jay
Lang.
Source: Cheeky
Monkey Vintage
Jewelry.

Starfish by Miriam Haskell.
Source: Patricia Hanten.

Cow Daisies.
Source: Jane Merrill.

Seven-petaled flower.
Source: Brenda's Treasures.

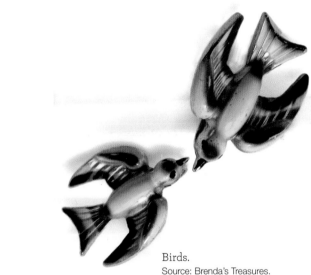

Birds.
Source: Brenda's Treasures.

Michael Todd's *Around the World in 80 Days* opened in several cities. In Boston, my parents sat behind Elizabeth Taylor, and my mother raved about her beauty: whatever rocks she had on suited her. However, my mother noted, also from behind in a London theater, that Princess Margaret's earrings seemed too heavy for her small face. I encouraged my mother to wear her gaudier stuff, and she did wear big rhinestone clips on occasion, but emphatically soignee. When Dior's "New Look" came in, she didn't go to extremes, but did wear more often a choker and pearls. I loved her cascades of dark blue and cognac rhinestones on white metal that were set so well that they seemed silken. They were swirled with gilt braid, which reminded me of my father's Navy dress uniforms. Often rearranging her jewelry box, I did not like the spikey vertical red-gold earrings and sunburst brooches from the Forties, but then they were history, not what she wore. If, as Schiaparelli said, women dress to be annoying to other women, that wasn't my mother, who preferred fitting in to getting attention.

When my father was based in Paris as a Navy liaison officer, my parents were invited to galas. A change of earrings! Now my mother wore Swarovski crystals for the evening parties. She made do with two floor-length gowns, white and peach, that she dyed pale blue and fire engine red to appear in something new one winter season. Once, at a nightclub, a stranger told her she looked like the Begum of some Middle Eastern country, and left a jeweled gold bracelet on the table in full view for her. Friends at the table told my mother to be flattered but she smarted and looked at the bracelet like a serpent. My father said it was probably intended for a dancer and my mother gave it to the maitre'd. The bracelet wouldn't have matched the rhinestones on white metal that, like those worn by Jane Russell and Marilyn Monroe in *Gentlemen Prefer Blondes*, cascaded from her ears, In fact, next to nothing of my mother's jewelry was "real"; some of her Swarovski bracelets and earrings she even lined with colored satin ribbons to match her gowns.

Wallace Simpson (1937).
Source: Hedda Walters, photographer,
Art Resource, New York.

Cushion-cut
sapphires.
Source: Lang Antique &
Estate Jewelry.

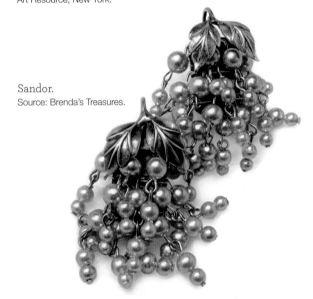

Sandor.
Source: Brenda's Treasures.

The Duchess of Chic

The Duke and Duchess of Windsor each felt the
other had given up a lot in the marriage: he lost the
crown and she lost her reputation. The Duchess mono-
gramed her bed sheets with "W&E," and the Duke liked
to see her in avant-garde earrings. Anna Sebba, the
Duchess of Windsor's biographer (*A Life of Simpson*),
enlightened me on the mid-century fashion icon's jewelry. "Wallis saw herself as a sovereign and a trendset-
ter. On the one hand, she loved her canary diamond
earrings, originally a gift from an Indian maharaja to
her husband's grandfather. They were immense; and
about them she said, 'I can't think of anything I would
rather have than these two diamonds.' But Wallis
was also a self-consciously gamine-type. Well before
meeting the Prince of Wales in the Twenties, she wore
mixes of semi-precious and precious stones, and asymmetrical designs, often striking yet jarring and theatrical, such as designs influenced by the Ballets Russes
and the Fauve painters. She wore both sides of the
street. With her hard-edged look she was elegant in the
designs of Suzanne Belperron, like a blue chalcedony
necklace with flowered clasp and matching earrings."

Citrines.
Source: Lang Antiques &
Estate Jewelry.

What about rumors she owned jewels, especially those of Queen Alexandra, not legitimately hers? Constance Coolidge who became the Comtesse de Jumilhac, stayed with Wallis immediately prior to her wedding, wrote to a mutual friend:

About those emeralds...Queen Alexandra never left any emeralds. The only emeralds in the royal family all belong to Queen Mary, who bought them or acquired them from the tsarina. She still has them. The Duke never had any jewels at all. He even had to buy his own silver when he went to Belvedere. The jewels that Wallis has are all new jewels he has bought for her here in Paris — some at Cartier's and mostly at Van Cleef & Arpels. She has lovely jewels but no great stones except her emerald engagement ring, which I find a little dark. I like her sapphire one better and also the diamond. The ruby is small. She has several sets of jewels but they are all modern. After all she would have told me if they had come from the royal family. I asked her and she said no — none of them, that the Duke had not been left any jewels at all.

Her taste settled on the latest costume jewelry because she wanted not to look like the royal family. Explained Anna Sebba:

It was always part of Wallis's make up to be different and cause a stir. But I think she had a good eye for bright color and big stones — and once she had money to go to couture houses for fabulous clothes she chose elegant, plain clothes that showed off her striking jewelry better. The subliminal message here is look what an elegant queen you'd have had if you had allowed me to live in England...but instead you have a frumpy monarch who wears funny flowery hats and fussy outfits.

The Duke gave her jewelry whenever he could but especially when he felt she had suffered a blow to make up for her humiliation at the hands of his own family. He could never give her enough to make up for what he felt she had given up — her good name, her freedom, her privacy, her life of party-giving, etc., to devote herself to him and live in exile as a demonized woman. He did not consider he had given up half as much as she had.

Patronizing numerous shops and designers, she often chose a set. The example Anna Sebba gives is the pale blue chalcedony sapphire and diamond necklace by Belperron c. 1935 (pre-marriage therefore). This was two rows of stained chalcedony beads — the same color as her blue eyes — the center set with a detachable cluster of cabochon sapphires and diamonds which could be worn as a brooch and with matching leaf-shaped ear clips. Almost everything was reset for her and she had a hand in designing some of her own earrings, including a collection of snail shell ear clips from the 1950s and 1960s.

The Duchess wore mostly clips of icy rhinestones, bright contrasting colors, and "often a carefree jumble of swirling shapes from this period. A transition was effected from the 1940s to 1950s towards lighter jewelry and from static to movement."

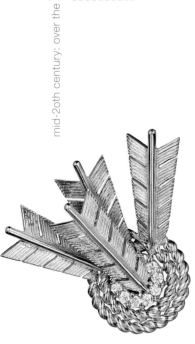

Target ear clips.
Source: Verdura.

Pearl and diamond ribbons.
Source: Lang Antique & Estate Jewelry.

The Duke of Chic

The word "fake" we could banish, along with pointing to our rhinestone and silver drops, and with deprecation saying they are "not real." Earrings made with creative design and craft need no gems or precious metal to be outstanding. "Imitation" we can reserve for the mindlessly mass-produced. Paradoxically, in times of scarcity of traditional precious materials, earring design takes off. One of the most sought-after fine jewelers of all-time eschewed diamonds and wasn't affected when platinum went to war as he preferred the buttery look of yellow gold for the extraordinary earrings he produced at this period.

An original jeweler and consummate artist, Fulco di Verdura had great success creating colorful jewelry that must have seemed loud at the time of white and white but had a heyday in the 40s and 50s, and retains its chic today. His glamorous jewelry was on the wild side, and his earrings had a mix of semi-precious stones, often big and cabochon, and sometimes natural objects like a seashell worked in.

Uniquely for a jeweler, Fulco was an aristocrat, a duke from Sicily (with a very long name), born in 1898 at his grandmother's house outside Palermo, into a family of artists and eccentrics limned by his cousin Giuseppe Lampedusa in the celebrated novel *The Leopard*. With a fun-loving personality, non-conformist temperament, and boundless creativity, his lifelong talent was connected with serving the upper echelon of society. In 1919, he first met Cole and Linda Porter when they were honeymooning in Sicily. He met Coco Chanel in 1925 when they were both at a party in Venice thrown by the Porters. After meeting Chanel, Fulco moved to Paris where he worked for her in textiles and ultimately designing jewelry for her. In the 1930s, he joined Paul Flato in Hollywood, and many actresses, including Marlene Dietrich, Greta Garbo, Joan Crawford, and Katherine Hepburn, wore his earrings, brooches, and bracelets.

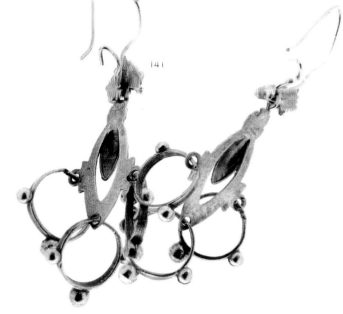

With backers Vincent Astor and Cole Porter, he opened his shop on Fifth Avenue in New York on September 1, 1939 — the same day war was declared in Europe.

With only word-of-mouth advertising, the business, today discreetly located on an upper floor of 712 Fifth Avenue, thrived. He had Astor on Wall Street to bring in the socialite clientele and Porter on Broadway to bring in the theater/Hollywood set. In the '40s and '50s, his stars were aligned, and women in America who couldn't get the European style from Europe became customers of Verdura.

During this time, he broke out on his own with designs that drew inspiration from his Sicilian childhood. In his earrings, he used forms from pomegranates to flaming hearts and Byzantine mosaics, classy and unsubtle at the same time. Sometimes he wrapped a form in gold braid, like nautical rope — like miniature Christo wrappings of the Reichstag or Pont Neuf — over the top. Because he came to jewelry as a designer, Fulco assumed that his jewelers could render any design into worthy objects. As Caroline Stetson of Verdura points out, his designs pushed the bench workers to the edge of their craftsmanship. If Fulco had grown up in the jewelry business, he might have had to tone down his designs to make them easier to fabricate.

Fulco, the man about town, was visible at The Stork Club and El Morocco, and in 1941, in Cole Porter's musical *Let's Face It*, Danny Kaye sang, "Liz Whitney has,

Cat Burglary

A movie cliché was the cat burglar. The wealthy used to have combination home safes that, in a very tense scene, a movie thief would crack. Of the many rich and famous celebrities who had real jewelry thefts, Sophia Loren was the most famous with regard to her loss and how she reacted. Crafty crook Peter Scott, sometimes called "The Gentleman Thief" because he was handsome, drove a Jaguar, never did anyone physical harm, and played a good game of tennis, decided to rob Loren. She was living in a rented house in London, while making a film adaptation of George Bernard Shaw's The Millionairess. Scott entered a ground floor window, went up the staircase into her bedroom suite, and pried open a tall cabinet that had a telltale padlock. Scott made off with a black case of suites of emeralds, rubies, sapphires, and diamonds, black pearls, and assorted rings, earrings, and bracelets, as well as souvenir black lingerie. On YouTube can be viewed the young Sophie Loren puffing on a cigarette and sighing as she spoke to television reporters about the May 29, 1960 robbery. She pointed her finger at the camera and said, "The thief will have no luck. I am a gypsy. I have cursed him." Her producer Pierre Rouve said the jewelry "means more than just wealth to Miss Loren — they were milestones on her struggles to success."

Scott hobnobbed with the highborn, went into their homes, and stole their jewels and cash. A pathological thief from childhood, he squandered Loren's jewels at the gambling tables on the French Riviera. He was jailed for fifteen years for successive convictions of theft.

A little over ten years later, Loren was robbed of another half-million dollars of jewelry when gunmen forced their way into a twenty-second-story apartment in Waldorf Towers, where she was staying while promoting another movie. Two young boys in New Jersey recovered some of the jewels in a brown paper bag. Like those jewels lost in Loren's prior theft, these were uninsured.

Declaring his passion for larceny finally ended, Peter Scott recounted his capers in his memoirs, lived in penury, and became a tennis coach.

on her bin of manure, a clip designed by the Duke of Verdura. Farming is so charming, they all say." Tyrone Power commissioned star-shaped earrings for his first wife Annabella, and Fulco embossed them a zircon "A" and "T."

The Duchess of Windsor had a conceit that she actually designed earrings that Fulco had created. When robbers got some of her jewelry, she went to Verdura to replace them. However, Fulco said he could not, as he could only do his own designs... checkmate! The two pairs she bought were all-purpose mabe pearls, one with diamonds set in a wire border and one crisscrossed with nautical rope. Fulco seemed to have got along with everybody, including the notoriously difficult Chanel, but the Duchess may not have been as favorite a client as Linda Porter or Babe Paley. During the Second World War, Churchill quipped that the Allies should send Fulco behind enemy lines in Sicily as an agent provocateur.

In 1985, seven years after Fulco's death, Ward Landrigan, the head of Sotheby's jewelry division, bought the Verdura business. Using the thousands of Fulco's drawings that had been carefully saved, Verdura creates opulent and breathtaking pieces today. I find I stare at these earrings, which seem perfection. The pairs that hang in my mind so I could draw them without looking are the multicolored zircon oak leaves and the diamond-encrusted bows, curling and rounded like real satin bows, over faceted oval white topaz. I also love the humor of his earrings of gold bands with diamonds on the inside, invisible from a distance and a treat to more intimate eyes. On the bowknot ear clips, a bit of gold ribbon and gold prongs add a typical *je ne sais quoi* Verdura touch.

Verdura never tired of the bowknot, whose ancestor is the *sevigne*, cousin to the girandole, popularized by Madame la Comtesse de Sevigne, the famous intellect and letter writer, in the seventeenth century. The countess said, "I fear nothing so much as a man who is witty all day long," yet wearing the fabric bow with pendant gems or pearls signaled she was witty pretty much nonstop. At the Carnavalet Museum in Paris hangs a portrait of the countess with the *sevigne* bowknot on her bodice. Ladies wanted to have the verve of this urbane lady so they, too, wore bows on their bosoms. Fulco's bowknots swell; they are asymmetrical and sculptural, with gems that tuck in the folds, quite invisible, as well as on the surface. They have an unpretentious, insouciant tenderness, like the letters the countess wrote her daughter faithfully in the provinces for thirty years, which Marcel Proust's fictional mother and grandmother, and college French majors like me, read. Aristocrats, from about 1850, no longer set the taste for earrings yet Fulco could reprise the bowknot to design exuberant brooches and ear clips.

Fulco said his earrings had the ability to make a woman look younger. Ward Landrigan explains that this results from a large surface of design and also, being clips, framing the face and complementing the intricate curves of the earlobe itself. "At Sotheby's, I didn't have to think how the earrings felt. The fact is that with a certain size earrings it's impractical to have them for pierced ears and, if made properly, the clip won't fall off. Now at Verdura, I see many women don't know how to wear the clips. I fondle earlobes daily as I point out the problem: they put the earrings on so the lobe wiggles. If you put the clip on far from the face, it snaps back — it's 'Earrings 101'. You don't hold a tray out in front of you when you are serving; you hold it close to your body." Fulco believed that earrings, being an important asset, needed volume. "Many women are given pea-sized earrings by their parents or a boy, which is regrettable. The Verdura earrings frame the face like a hat. A lot of women are afraid to wear the more exciting earrings, but look at Diana Vreeland — she was not even very good looking but she called attention to herself dramatically."

Flares by Suzanne Belperron.
Source: Ward Landrigan.

Belperron

Jewelry history has a heroine and she designed earrings. Suzanne Belperron was doing arty fine jewelry when the Nazis occupied France. She purchased the business from her partner, Bernard Herz, in January 1941 in order to preserve it, since it was illegal for a Jew to own a business in occupied Paris. Herz was deported to a concentration camp, where he died, and his son Jean was taken prisoner of war. Suzanne Belperron held the company under her name until 1945 when Jean returned and she resumed the partnership with him; the company was then called Jean Herz-Suzanne Belperron. She was later awarded a Legion of Honor for her efforts in the Resistance during the war. In her private salon were customers like Colette, the Duchess of Windsor, Elsa Schiaparelli (the first to tout Belperron), and later Frank Sinatra and Gary Cooper. Her pieces were unsigned — the style she maintained haughtily was her signature — but often seen in *Vogue* and *Harper's Bazaar*. Because she was very pretty, Man Ray photographed her for the French *Vogue*. Ward Landrigan bought the drawings privately in 1999 from her heirs. Suzanne Belperron's curvy chalcedony leaves veined with silver are feminine, playful, and would look great on us if we could only put them on. Mr. Landrigan pointed to an interesting feature of her having been a jeweler who also wore her earrings. "The only unique back was a spoon design by Suzanne. She made hard-stone earrings and the little clip designed by men would hurt, so she replaced it with the softer contour of a spoon."

Blue Flowers by Suzanne Belperron.
Source: Ward Landrigan.

Autumn leaves by Suzanne Belperron. Source: Ward Landrigan.

Small blueberry clusters.
Source: Brenda's Treasures.

Carmen Miranda

In summer, my mother wore earrings that were miniature brimmed straw hats, with bunches of glass fruit, à la Carmen Miranda. A hat maker, Carmen Miranda made her tutti-frutti signature hat after the hats on African-American sellers in the market. Only five feet tall, she made preposterous and adorable hats...and they called for proportionately crazy earrings. In films or while performing on stage, from her ears dangled glass bunches of tropical fruit and big, light jewelry, including papier-mâché. For instance, when Carmen wore leaf-motif earrings, they were catalpas and, if she had on shells, they could be as big as conches or lobster claws — and then have festive glass beads and flowers hanging from them. The stage and television shows of her and Hawaiian girls in leis, or a mariachi band, dancing with wild abandon, gave many American women inspiration to stray from convention in their dress and lives. They wore halter-tops, sarongs, and dramatic turbans. Their ears were partially covered by headdresses to go to a nightclub — only the bottom rim of the ear in view with happy and flamboyant earrings, such as faux shells or big blossoms of kid leather that were soft as butter and cleverly twisted and sewn into miniature orchids, lilies, hibiscus, and dogwood. They swept upward and downward and were like corsages for ears.

Moon gods by
Joseff of Hollywood.
Source: Connie Glass

Joseff of Hollywood

In the Golden Era of Hollywood studios, one jeweler, above all others, catered to the movies' need for glitz. Eugene Joseff moved as a young man from Chicago to the West Coast. His wife, after she finished at UCLA, walked into his office looking for a job, fell in love with him, and never left. She would carry on the business after his tragic death, at 48, in a plane crash. In a 1948 article in *Movie Show*, he says the most useful piece of jewelry is the brooch and after that "earrings should be the next jewelry of investment. They also have many uses. You can wear them on your hat, cuffs, shoes, as well as your ears." Few of us would put these uses into practice, but it made sense because the Joseff of Hollywood earrings were show-stoppers and hardly an "accessory."

Joseff's importance as a force in mid-century jewelry began when he worked on a 1934 movie *The Affairs of Celliini,* about the life of Benvenuto Cellini. He faulted the jewelry as modern that Constance Bennett wore with the authentic period costumes. He said he could do better, and for the next fifteen years he analyzed old jewelry to reproduce for the movies. His jewelry appeared in *Camille* (1937), *Gone with the Wind* — the amethyst necklace, bracelet, and earring set worn by Vivian Leigh, (1939), *Samson and Delilah* (1949), and *Ben Hur* (1959). He often used a finish called Russian or antique gold, to be less reflective under bright studio lights.

It's a secret where the collection of the firm's jewelry is now warehoused. Because the studios rented and did not buy the jewelry, it's a gigantic trove of necklaces, brooches, tiaras, earrings, and also bejeweled daggers, cigarette cases, and so forth. The first choice of my daughters and me to see from one of the little black velvet rectangular boxes in the warehouse would be Marilyn Monroe's pearls from an ultimate movie about jewelry, *Gentlemen Prefer Blondes.*

Liz

In fact, it was in the movie *Gentlemen Prefer Blondes* that Marilyn Monroe, with diamonds cascading from her lobes, sang "Diamonds are a girl's best friend" — a saying that found its ultimate believer in Elizabeth Taylor. Husbands Mike Todd, Richard Burton, and even Eddie Fisher showered Elizabeth Taylor with gifts from Bulgari and Cartier — gifts that were national news, such as when Burton bought a diamond for over a million dollars from Cartier, the highest price to date for a diamond; then when Liz had Cartier design a necklace featuring it, as a security measure, three men with identical suitcases delivered the necklace to the Burton yacht, which was anchored in Monaco, and detectives carrying machine guns escorted Liz and Richard to Princess Grace's fortieth birthday party.

In his novel *Jewelry Talks*, Richard Klein writes of Elizabeth Taylor's "royal lust for jewelry":

> *From an early age, and she was a phenomenally precocious star, she wanted only the biggest and the most prestigious stones, only the greatest jewelry: the Cartier diamond, the Peregrina pearl, the Schlumberger Iguana brooch, the diamond plumes of the Prince of Wales*

During her acquisitive period, I see Liz as a dancing Kali wearing a garland of husband heads. Her last husband catalogued the gems in a book that he showed guests. Why men felt compelled to give her these jewels is interesting. They were fascinated by her violet eyes, but must have felt her unsatisfied, unsated. They wanted to make her happy and participated in the fantasy that vast expenditure can bring great happiness. When the relationship foundered, she fled with the big expensive jewels. The Christie's auction of her jewelry collection in December 2011 set a world record for the most valuable private collection of jewels sold at auction.

Rainbow "balls," diamond and multicolored sapphire clips, by JAR, Paris, formerly in the collection of Elizabeth Taylor.
Source: John Bigelow Taylor.

Ruby girandoles, formerly in the collection of Elizabeth Taylor.
Source: John Bigelow Taylor.

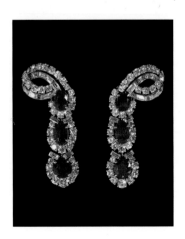

Cartier ruby drops, formerly in the collection of Elizabeth Taylor.
Source: John Bigelow Taylor.

From the collection, the chandelier style of earrings stands out because she could wear these prodigious baubles that few could. The white cultured pear pearl and diamond chandeliers, and the marquis cluster and gold pair, were breathtaking and must have flared stupendously when she turned her face and head. Nevertheless, I admired most the daring colored pairs of chandeliers by Van Cleef & Arpels, especially the pink coral and diamond ones with a completely excess touch of deep purple amethyst drops appended below the traditional chandeliers.

An amazing footage appears on YouTube of the intimate moment in August 1957 when Mike Todd gave Liz a ruby necklace and matching dangling earrings. They were three months married, she was pregnant, they had rented a villa outside of Monte Carlo, and, wearing a tiara, Liz was swimming laps. Mike came over to the pool to surprise her with the boxes from Cartier. We see him put the ruby necklace around her neck, and then Liz adorns herself with the dangling earrings. Only when she has both on, as if to say "Now I'm dressed," she flutters her lashes and looks from side to side to be admired.

Since there was no mirror, Liz looked in the pool to see her reflection. A woman who enjoyed her bling, she recalled, "The jewelry was so glorious, rippling red on blue like a painting...I just shrieked with joy, put my arms around Mike's neck, and pulled him into the pool after me."

Liz would describe this as a perfect summer day and perfect day of love. In the footage, behind her in the pool, we glimpse Eddie Fisher, literally treading water. Security was already having the next husband lined up.

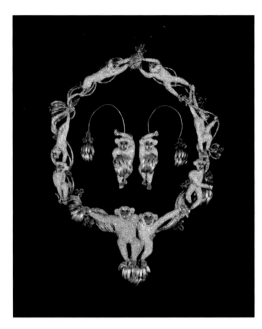

Bejeweled monkeys,
formerly in the collection of
Elizabeth Taylor
Source: John Bigelow Taylor.

Tassels by Marina Bulgari,
formerly in the collection of
Elizabeth Taylor.
Source: John Bigelow Taylor.

Coral, diamonds and amethyst,
formerly in the collection of
Elizabeth Taylor.
Source: John Bigelow Taylor.

South Sea cultured pearls and diamonds,
collection of Elizabeth Taylor.
Source: John Bigelow Taylor.

Belted hemispheres
by Trifari.
Source: Rose Marie
Reynolds of Vintage
Crown Trifari.

Young Queen Elizabeth II

The parents of Princess Elizabeth, King George VI and Queen Elizabeth, gave her a spectacular pair of earrings as a wedding present in 1947. These were long chandeliers with three drops reputedly displaying every modern cut of diamond. She must have looked at them with initial dismay as they were for pierced ears. A practical girl, she had her ears pierced — and this prompted many women of her generation to follow suit.

Elizabeth's father also gave her a second wedding present of a sapphire suite: a long necklace of oblong sapphires surrounded by diamonds (which she would shorten) and a pair of matching squire sapphire earrings also bordered with diamonds, dating from 1850. Elizabeth II did what royalty has always done — goodbye to the old styles and hello to the new. She was also given gifts left and right, another tradition. For her coronation, the people of Brazil gave her a necklace and earrings of large square-cut aquamarines set in a ribbon-chain necklace of diamonds. What's a girl to do? Later, she had a tiara made and later Brazil gave her a bracelet to complete the set.

Mamie

My mother held her own in the game of bridge. As a young Navy wife, she played with the First Lady, Mamie Eisenhower. She praised Mamie for her lack of snobbery and her chic style. Mamie, who favored the New Look, wore Trifari costume jewelry of pearls and diamonds for the inaugural balls of 1953 and 1957, the first to complement her sleeveless, neck-less "Mamie pink" gown and the second for her yellow-gold gown. Clearly, when a First Lady bought jewelry available at J.C. Penney and Woolworth's, it was okay for the wives of upper echelon military and government to wear costume jewelry in the evening too.

Jackie

The icon for the late 1950s is a woman of impeccable and conservative taste, Jacqueline Kennedy. JFK liked to see her with upswept hair and in long drop earrings. The first anniversary gift from the then-Senator in 1954 was a pair of floral black pearl drops, which he presented the night before their anniversary date in what would become a lifelong custom of exchanging gifts in a private setting. Jackie returned to Tiffany's a year later and had them make them interchangeable and added a white pearl. Sometimes she wore the studs with no pearls. In 1956, Jack gave her a birthday gift of gold and diamond earrings; the uppermost stone was heart-shaped. Two years later he gave her an identical pair in platinum.

Heliotrope
necklace and
earrings by Trifari.
Source: Rose Maria
Reynolds of Vintage
Crown Trifari Jewelry.

Art Earrings

A few iconoclasts of means have worn the jewelry made by famous artists — Calder and Dali's creations are notable.

Alexander Calder (1898–1976) crafted 1,800 pieces of jewelry over the course of his career. He made them of the same materials — brass, gold and steel with bits of glass, wood, and ceramic — as the pieces of his circus at the Whitney Museum. One Calder pair spells out a surrealist pun Jean Miro made in the '20s, "A bas la Mediterranée" (At the bottom of/Down with the Mediterannean). This pair, sweet and manifestly humorous, has childlike lettering that practically twinkles at many different levels, reminding me of alphabet soup. The pair is so obviously handcrafted the effect is as fresh now as when some admirer of the artist walked out wearing them in the 1940s (or perhaps as early as 1937). Because Calder rarely used solder, the parts of his jewelry move freely and unpredictably. He used a lot of spirals and linked strips of metal with loops, which he riveted, or bound, with fine wire.

Dali designed but did not make fashion earrings himself. The designer Schiaparelli commissioned his earliest jewelry. His many items included a diamond-encrusted heart brooch and earrings, dripping ruby blood, and a ruby and diamond "Honeycomb Heart" brooch and matching earrings that were a surreal joke on being a sweetheart.

Telephone receivers — each of them a curving receiver with an organic form, with little ruby and emerald jewels hanging like speech — are my favorite of his earrings. He subtitled them "The persistence of sound" and described them as follows: "The ear is a symbol of harmony and unity; the telephone design a reminder of the speed of modern communication — the hope and danger of instantaneous exchange of thought."

Feathery red necklace and earrings by Trifari.
Source: Rose Maria Reynolds of Vintage Crown Trifari Jewelry.

Fenestrated by Trifari.
Source: Rose Maria Reynolds of Vintage Crown Trifari Jewelry.

Dahlias by Trifari.
Source: Rose Maria Reynolds of Vintage Crown Trifari Jewelry.

Berry cluster wing-backs by Trifari.
Source: Rose Marie Reynolds of Vintage Crown Trifari Jewelry.

Designing Earrings Outside the Box

By Cathleen McCarthy

Earrings present a particular challenge when it comes to designing "outside the box." Not only do they have to match, or at least correlate design-wise, they must also be relatively lightweight, if the designer expects them to be worn. Necklaces and bracelets hang from sturdy parts of the skeleton — the neck and wrist. Rings are supported by another, our fingers, and a brooch can be pinned to a lapel, but earrings dangle from fragile bits of flesh, our earlobes.

Much as we might like to dangle fabulous sculptures and chunky gemstones from our ears, there's a weight limit for that delicate body part. As the Bible says, "The spirit is willing, but the flesh is weak."

If the earring attaches via piercing, as is most common these days, the hole in the flesh is going to be noticeably stretched unless a designer covers that with a button closure — adding even more weight to the proposition. If a heavy earring attaches via clip, that clip has to squeeze pretty tight to the earlobe to keep from sliding off under the weight. Ouch. No wonder celebrities on the red carpet often forego "statement earrings" for the "statement necklace."

I once interviewed an enamel artist who had become famous for his art jewelry. His enameling was breathtaking, wildly creative, and perfectly crafted, but when he invited me to try on a pair of his enameled gold earrings at the Manhattan gallery that represented him, I thought they were going to rip my ears off. I couldn't get them off fast enough. Yet women were lining up to buy them. They were "collectible." I never saw anyone actually wearing them.

Most famous sculptors and artists who try their hands at designing jewelry start (and often end) with a necklace, a brooch, a ring, or a bracelet — one-offs with relatively few design restraints. But a few brave souls go on to attempt the challenge of designing earrings, those twin sculptures that attach to the lobe and frame the face.

In addition to Calder and Dali, Man Ray was one of the few visionaries who attempted — and beautifully managed — to reinvent the earring in the last century. Bespoke designers such as Joel Arthur Rosenthal, known as JAR, have also designed mismatched and oversized earrings that sell for hundreds of thousands at auction.

Others have been less successful at creating eye-catching ear ornaments that were actually wearable by a human being with nerve endings, but who could blame them for trying? Earrings are one of the most noticeable pieces of jewelry anyone can wear. They're the first ornament someone sees when they look at your face. For this reason, women were keen to buy Man Ray's famous gold spirals. The French actress Catherine Deneuve was famously photographed with his giant sculptures hanging from her ears, no visible sign of pain on her beautiful face. The secret? Well, she was an actress! However, Man Ray — or, more likely, Gem Montebello, the Italian jeweler that actually created the earrings from the artist's sketch — designed a hook that fit over the outside of the ear so the weight and bulk of the earring were supported by the ear itself, that is the cartilage, rather than the earlobe. You can't see this hook behind Deneuve's lustrous blonde mane.

There was no such clever mechanism behind the oversized, hammered brass earrings Calder was making before World War II. Calder also made dozens of smaller, more practical earrings, given that jewelry paid his bills as he

built his reputation as a sculptor and fine artist, but let's face it — those tiny hammered spirals weren't going to get his wealthy patrons noticed.

When avant-garde collectors such as Mary Rockefeller and Peggy Guggenheim wore a piece of Calder into a cocktail party, they expected heads to turn. Guggenheim claimed she was the only one willing to sacrifice her lobes to this quest. "Every woman in New York who is fortunate enough to be decorated by a Calder jewel has a brooch or a bracelet or a necklace," she once wrote. "I am the only woman in the world who wears his enormous mobile earrings."

The earrings Guggenheim refers to were in the Calder Jewelry exhibition at the Philadelphia Museum of Art in 2008 — and she wasn't kidding when she said "enormous." Made from hammered sterling, they measured six inches long and almost five inches wide. I didn't lift them, but I couldn't imagine hanging them from my ears. However, Calder was famous for inventing the mobile and, if you wanted a recognizable Calder, you wore mobiles-for-the-ears. It wouldn't be the first time a woman put up with intense pain in order to turn heads.

Calder was famously influenced by African tribal art and jewelry, and certain tribes have been putting up with that kind of pain for centuries in order to ornament their bodies. In fact, many tribes purposely expanded the piercings in their earlobes until they could fit plugs measuring several inches across. Not too many of us are willing to go that far.

Regardless of the toll they may take on our lobes, however, shoulder-grazing earrings go in and out of style. Dramatically chunky danglers have been showing up again lately in runway shows and red carpet events. There is an art to carving gems so they look substantial but don't weigh a ton, and it works best with opaque gems.

As for precious metals, one way to minimize weight without sacrificing size is to build earrings around a hollow structure. Stanley Lechtzin perfected this technique, known as electroforming, in the late '60s and early '70s, which allowed for some highly-sophisticated goldsmithing around hollow, deceptively lightweight ornaments. His Torque series is a great example.

Filigree is a more time-tested way to increase size without increasing weight. Greek and Etruscan jewelers were making dramatic, intricate filigree earrings from gold wire as early as the sixth century B.C. Not only did this delicate, open metalwork mean they could make earrings bigger and more elaborate, they could do it with a relatively tiny amount of precious metal. With the cost of gold at an all-time high — nearly $1,700 an ounce — the art of filigree is due for a major comeback.

For fashion earrings, the sky's the limit in terms of materials — and, therefore, so is size, shape, and color. Aluminum is lightweight, so is polymer clay, Swarovski crystal, and plastic. You can get a lot of drama with minimal weight out of many kinds of wood, seeds, and coral.

Type in "lightweight earrings" on Etsy and all kinds of crazy, creative ear ornaments pop up. It's refreshingly clear that the quest to design earrings "outside the box" is alive and well — and the possibilities are endless.

Cathleen McCarthy is a freelance writer whose stories on jewelry design and history, as well as travel and business, appear in many national magazines and on her blog, TheJewelryLoupe.com.

Chunky cognac.
Source: Hancocks of London.

Red gold clusters.
Source: Hancocks of London.

A Premier Designer

The top costume jewelry designers manufactured at different levels, with the top level selling at Saks Fifth Avenue and the like. Their creations had much handwork. Glass stones were made in Europe, often exclusive so that other jewelers could not use the same stones. High-end glass stones were set in bezels just like gemstones. Sometimes manufacturers can be identified by clips, which were unique to that brand. Alfred Philippe was a premier designer and Rose Reynolds of Vintage Crown Jewelry, who specializes in his creations, says:

My interest in Costume Jewelry grew out of a love of dressing up and wearing my mom's jewelry in the late 1950s. It was a very happy time.

When I looked around for something to do after we closed our antique shop in 1999, I decided to focus on something that delighted me. Costume jewelry filled the bill. However, after a few years, I realized there were only a couple of manufacturers who consistently made really beautiful jewelry. Boucher, Ciner, Pennino, Mazer and early Coro were candidates.

But for true design brilliance and longevity only Alfred Philippe existed for me. His own designs and the ones he coached from other talented people are what makes Crown Trifari my very favorite of all. His rigorous education in design made him pay attention to every detail and by the 1950s he had streamlined many of his designs so thousands of women could enjoy wearing beautiful jewelry, some of which kept one guessing if it was real or not. In this way his genius lives on, because up to 80 years later, the jewelry still exists and is lovingly repaired or restored by people like me.

Eugene Jewelry.
Source: Brenda's Treasures.

Diamond-shaped with sapphires.
Source: Lang Antique & Estate Jewelry.

Sophisticated women of mid-century treated their earrings as their single, most important item of jewelry, the element that called attention to their eyes — made them look bigger and brought out their eye color as well. Faux was as good as real because it looked as good and, once cocktail jewelry (iconized by John Cheever and quite likely invented by Verdura) came into vogue, many felt they shouldn't go out...anywhere... without their earrings.

In Verdura's tradition of the bowknot.
Source: Verdura.

Hanging Cool:
The 1960s

*I*n 1964, *Time Magazine* discerned a trend among college girls for ear-piercing. At my prep school, we did not pierce our ears — it would have been an offense, like wearing fluffy sweaters or the color chartreuse. My friend Susan Robertson came back from Radcliffe with pierced ears — this seemed fitting for an intrepid Cliffie whose grandfather was the first to climb Mt. Everest, who had already summered in Pakistan, and who would climb as an avocation herself. In 1966, *Cosmopolitan* described piercing as chic and feminine; the obverse was true, that earrings with volume and big stones were passé.

Wearing big gemstone clip earrings clinched Mrs. Robinson (Anne Bancroft, then 36) as an "older woman" when Benjamin Braddock and she begin their *pas de deux* (Dustin Hoffman, only six years younger, playing Benjamin, the younger man) in *The Graduate* (1967).

In *The Graduate*, Mrs. Robinson lures young Benjamin into her unlit empty house and up to a bedroom. While Benjamin is trying to withdraw and Mrs. Robinson is denying seducing him, she pinions him in her daughter's bedroom: "Mrs. Robinson, you're trying to seduce me."

She rubs her earlobe where the Harry Winston ear clips had been. "Well, no, I hadn't thought of it." But then she casts her earrings like two sparkling dice onto the frilly bedspread.

Benjamin, jumping out of his skin from nerves, hears noises downstairs and escapes to the first floor, in time to greet a hale and hearty Mr. Robinson, Benjamin's father's business partner. The seduction attempt is foiled, but Benjamin's libido is awakened and, inevitably, they try again. This time he gets a hotel room and she sits in the bar. He is a virgin, and she is excited too: she removes the earring that is getting in the way as he calls from the lobby and they exchange directions. The earrings don't go back on as she leaves the bar for the tryst.

Yves St. Laurent and model.
Source: The Image Works.

Anne Bancroft conveys her character by what she wants. Those earring ear clips were a statement of Mrs. Robinson's intimidation. A woman Benjamin's age was not wearing anything of that high sparkle!

Until we had committed to pierce each other's ears with a sterilized needle, ice cubes, and half a raw potato behind each ear, we talked about piercing with our friends but avoided clip-ons. Nobody should know our cowardice. Like Pinocchio, we tried to hide our ears — usually under the curtain of hair — and for jobs, long nails were out for secretaries. Playboy Bunnies and stewardesses also did not accentuate their ears.

It would be 1971 before I went through the ritual. I was living in Iran and wanted to wear gold studs. Wow, now I could wear earrings and talk on the phone at the same time!

Within a few years multiple piercings were the wild thing to do and single piercings took a back seat. Yet, for a decade, coinciding with the 1960s, attention was completely directed to the phenomenon of wearing earrings as opposed to what you wore. Did we notice if someone wore studs or a little ring? Hardly!

Most girls gradually ceded to having pierced ears, as outlandish as it seemed when we first heard of the practice. Now, as before, earrings were clues where you belonged. At the turn of the century mostly immigrants from southern Europe wore them; you had to wear clips or threaded screw-backs to be an "old American." Now girls either went forward and had their ears pierced, or went without, because few by 1965 wanted to have clip or screw closures, which "said" conservative. Virtually all a girl had to do to identify with the anti-materialist youth culture was pierce her ears. Ironically, though, you couldn't see that Joan Baez wore earrings until decades later under all that flowing hair and Cher, who would wear earrings with va-va-vroom and extra tiers in the 1970s, was in hippie vests and bellbottoms — and no ears in view in the '60s.

If you didn't have a poor lottery number and have to fight in Vietnam, the 1960s were a wonderful time to be young. That's why we used words like cool, groovy, and far-out so much. Self-expression was our mantra and we were reinventing the world, though, as I recall, when it came to the bolder strokes, many bright girls masked our insecurities under being the chick or moll to the empowered young male. Between travels abroad, I went to graduate school. In one Master's program, we spent a week in a corrugated cardboard factory, constructing classroom furniture with power handsaws and industrial glue. I took a course whose final was to fill a trash can with objects that would awaken the mind — groovy!

In the late 1960s to the early '70s, a youthful counterculture took in a broad swath of the population and the outsider impulse dominated. We dressed like flower children or hippies not merely to shock our parents, but as a visible extension of keeping our spirits free. We wore earrings to support the crafts of people who lived on the margins of society (many of us were attempting this) and people unseen or whom we met on travels to the Third World. We pierced our ears because our parents didn't want us to. We traveled to remote places, and long, flowing skirts and earrings were things we could bring home, like talismans of a simpler, more authentic life.

A whole generation went on stage in a sacred play being devised as we went along. The audience for this pan-society happening was the people of yesterday — like our parents — waiting for the characters and plot we would reveal. We entertained them with sass, bravura, dress, and satire of what had been, what we understood they had been. We were masterminding an unfettered culture founded on openness, rejection of the war impulse, and an embrace of global cultural awareness. The last is where adornment became so important. Some of us trekked around other lands and returned wearing their apparel — mysterious beads, mirrored blouses, sculpted sandals, and all manner of exotic adornment worn in those places traditionally. We developed a firm taste, an eye, for the handmade along the way.

In the late 1960s, my husband and I lived in Iran for our personal goals, focally his academic research on Shi'a Islam. In the seventeenth century, Shah Abbas had brought a clock-maker from Switzerland and put him under house arrest, to remain in Isfahan and keep the clock in good working order. Similarly, Mohammed Reza Shah Pahlavi (1919–1980), in the high point of his rule, hosted experts ranging from Israeli agronomists to develop large-scale farming, to engineers to modernize Iran's television studios. These experts and their families lived in gated communities with their pools and staff, and clubs and R&R trips back to the West. I saw them only if their children attended the international school where I taught.

Although we stopped by the American embassy for an occasional burger, we spent most of our leisure time in Tehran's wondrous central bazaar, located in the south of the city. There a car was useless, i.e., streets were for people and animal-drawn carts. A stranger could easily miss the entrance to a cavernous extent of walkways and shops covering several blocks. Plastic products, by some common consent, stayed at the periphery while inside the labyrinth every tall cake of sugar, pile of turmeric, display of fabrics, weavings, jewelry, or metalwork pulled the eye to open stalls, usually arranged by type of wares. A blue haze filtered

Mary Ann Scherr topaz and silver.
Source: Mary Ann Scherr.

Mary Ann Scherr gold mobiles.
Source: Mary Ann Scherr.

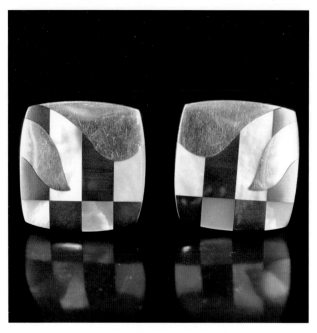

Tiffany checkerboards.
Source: Hancocks of London.

through, punctuated by columns of golden light where you could take your prospective purchase for a closer look. The Istanbul bazaar was a madhouse and the Lahore bazaar a festival, but an air of subdued mystery and archaic glamour clung to the Tehran bazaar.

Bargaining in the bazaar was a ritual game of wits. A raised eyebrow, tongue click, or sigh were signs to be read. Elaborate formalities called *ta'arof* opened the bargaining. This was followed by innocuous chitchat as tea glasses were filled and refilled until the seller's helper brought in fruit and pastries on a silver tray. There was little local interest in the antiquities for sale in the bazaar, with the important exception of carpets. Carpet sellers were the princes and they overwhelmed the inexperienced shopper by slapping down carpet after carpet, old and new, in piles several feet high. By contrast, the antiquarians who sold old brass and copper and old jewelry attracted few customers yet required proof of interest before pulling out drawers of their best stock.

First, they drew our attention to tin, hand-painted cigarette-holders, enameled brooches, and earrings *en*

Textured gold domes with off-center diamonds.
Source: Lang Antiques & Estate Jewelry.

Artist palettes, black opals with star-set rubies and sapphires.
Source: Lang Antiques & Estate Jewelry.

Catherine Deneuve wearing Man Ray
lampshade earrings.
Source: Man Ray Trust.

Golden
Cleopatras.
Source: Bruce Snell.

Tear drops from Palm Springs.
Source: Jane Merrill.

Emerald acorns.
Source: The Three Graces.

tremblant or with miniature painting on mother-of-pearl. These were made expressly as tourist items as middle-class Iranian women, familiar with European and American styles, favored small, gold pierced earrings and nothing dangly, lest they looked tribal. I bought a mosaic-inlaid wood box and three pairs of earrings. One pair had dozens of multicolored glass seed beads, hanging from a triangular surmount and looking like a bead curtain. A very showy pair of white silver filigree in the shape of lozenges had one pale round dot of lapis at the tip. Both pairs were wearable, the second probably made for foreigners. The third pair, for a bride, the seller said, were the size of Christmas ornaments, dark silver, with agate and turquoise. The agate was earthy and bright and the earrings seemed like a sampler of metalwork — braiding, granulation, stamping, and etching — all on their Aladdin's lamp shape.

The designs of the 1960s bucked conventions of jewelry technique. Seaman Schepps accented white turbo shells with gold or substituted wood for gold as a setting. Silversmiths like Carl Tasha were forging and fusing instead of hammering from metal sheets. Mod designers made big flat mobiles in light plastic, black and white op art, or "Day-Glo" almost phosphorescent colors. In 1968, at a street fair in Cambridge, Massachusetts, I bought a pair of earrings made of small nails twisted, hammered, and fused like early Kenneth Jay Lane chandelier earrings of hammered metal in the collection of the Metropolitan Museum. Sometimes our '60s earrings were as campy as floppy fabric daisies or as homely as beads on rawhide; others seemed to me Mobius-magical, like faceted Lucite balls and parabolas.

The earrings moved fetchingly in space and swished with our long straight hair, but hairstyles, as always in history, held sway over earrings. At Woodstock in 1969, the girls wore beaded headbands or kerchiefs and necklaces, but if they wore earrings (and they likely did, wearing studs or dangling beads) they are not visible. I had a blue spiral pair that bounced like a pogo stick, miniature Slinky toy metal ones, chrome and black plastic

Seamans Schlepps
turbo shell.
Source: Lang Antique &
Estate Jewelry.

chain pendants, and a rhinestone and white vinyl pair
of concentric rings. After our girlhoods of being proper
— at Wellesley College, we received demerits if we wore
jeans or shorts to the town, and at Mount Holyoke, before
a dance the girls had to demonstrate their skirt length
when they sat in a chair — we wore cute little dresses with
little underwear that liberated us from the constraints.

The op-art movement and handcrafted silver seem to
me in retrospect the most exciting vis-à-vis earrings. I wish
I could see now the meticulous silver bobs sold in Harvard
Square then and imagine feeling like a sun wearing a solar
system in each ear. The gulf between conventional status
jewelry and what we liked and wore — the mod jewelry, the
ethnic style or international pieces from North Africa and
India as well as what we made ourselves of glass beads
and wire — was never clearer than when we paged through
the ritzy magazines. There we saw the "old lady" styles
from fancy jewelers with their encrustations of jewels and
their whimsical birds and animals. Emerald frog earrings
with red ruby eyes? The counterculture disdained both
opulence and the kind of whimsy that men imposed, which
suggested that women were frilly and silly. Yet, in our
hometowns, Avon and Sarah Coventry were doing a brisk
business of direct-selling at home jewelry parties while in
the boutiques of Paris and on Fifth Avenue in Manhattan,
the trade was probably unaffected by our ideology.

High Fashion Rebel

Diane Vreeland's tenure at *Vogue* coincided with the
1960s. Joining *Vogue* in 1962, she thoroughly shook up
the old guard. Reigning for a decade, before she was fired
and became a consultant to the Metropolitan Museum
Costume Institute, she wore long tassel earrings that
dropped all the way down to her chest. Model Lauren Hutton wears only one tassel in her ear on a '60s *Vogue* cover.
Good ideas reassert and Yuri Ichihashi creates elegant
tassels après Diane Vreeland today.

Inlaid enamel with globes.
Source: The Three Graces.

Jackie II

We recollect the perfect Cassini suits and pillbox hats of the campaign wife, strapless classy ball gowns, and the black sweater and white trousers, with sunglasses, of the working urbanite. With nearly whatever she wore went earrings that looked great with that full dark hair, lovely eyes, high cheekbones, and wide face.

The first night Jackie became a lover to Aristotle Onassis, he looked into her jewelry case. What he saw took him aback — to his eyes trifling — and he immediately called Van Cleef & Arpels to send to his yacht something worthy of his new inamorata. Unless someone plans to cash in gifts of jewelry in old age, the jewelry is personal to her, the result of her magpie's eye, and its value based on meaning and beauty, not price tag. When the contents of Jackie's Fifth Avenue apartment were auctioned by Sotheby's in 1996, her friend Kenneth Jay Lane said "she was not that interested in valuable jewelry — she left the good stuff at the bank."

Lane's creations were well-represented at the sale — the fashionable floral and naturalistic costume designs, striking but ladylike, to wear day or night, that my mother called "cocktail jewelry."

Jackie also wore fake pearls and mixed costume jewelry with real jewelry. Her trademark was elegant simplicity and she often accessorized her European chic couture with a whimsical touch. The costume jewelry, to be sure, was often "designer," like the silvered metal ball ear clips by Yves Saint Laurent and faux emerald and diamond ear clips by Chanel. Kenneth Jay Lane designed specifically for Jackie. Among those pairs were pearlescent conches with gold accent, black glass baroque "pearls" topped with rhinestone pavé, and hoops with sparkles, looking like curved bamboo. She seems to have worn the shells when Caroline christened the naval carrier USS *John F. Kennedy* in 1967 and the black glass ear clips with a simple white dress when she met Charles De Gaulle in 1961.

After the 1960 election, JFK gave her an emerald set she wore to the Inaugural Ball. She wore the necklace and 1-1/4" top and drop earrings separately and together on many occasions. When Kennedy was a senator, he gave her a pair of crystal waterfalls to celebrate the birth of Caroline in 1957. These became a signature accessory and she wore them to Paris as First Lady. They, too, had removable drop pendants. For all of her demure air and little girl voice, Jackie was, to paraphrase Coco Chanel, a woman on the move and as such she liked top and drop earrings versatile for travel or several occasions in a day.

She liked the white enamel and gold clips she called her "banana earrings"; Bunny Mellon, with whom she carried out redecoration of the White House, gave them to her. Jackie had David Webb make her a similar pair with cobalt blue enamel.

Ari liked to have his presents of jewelry delivered deep in a bouquet of flowers or on a breakfast tray. The engagement bouquet had a flowery diamond and emerald necklace and leafy earrings. His nuptial gift of a Van Cleef & Arpels ruby heart necklace — diamonds set in gold flowers, with a ruby hanging from each flower — came with heart-shaped ruby ear clips surrounded by diamonds. Jackie understood absolutely that less is more. Wearing these to the Metropolitan Museum Costume Institute gala in 1979 with a dark strapless gown, she had no other adornment.

Jackie also wore Schlumberger's naturalistic three-dimensional jewelry and, after her marriage to Onassis, Van Cleef & Arpels (from the vastly expensive to the little gold Chinese mask motif pair). For her fortieth birthday, either from Ari or Van Cleef, she received unique earrings to commemorate the *Apollo 11* mission to the moon. In *Jackie Oh!*, Kitty Kelley described them as "a sapphire-studded earth at the ear and a large ruby moon hanging from a chain. The Apollo ship was attached to a thin gold thread which circled the sapphire earth and then dropped to the ruby moon."

Gold Waffles.
Source: Hancocks of London.

Optic art earrings by
Wendy Ramshaw and David
Watkins (c. 1960s). Gift of
the artists, 2001.
Source: The Museum of Arts &
Design, New York. John Bigelow
Taylor, photographer.

By Phillip Fike (1968). Gift of the
Johnson Wax Company through the
American Crafts Council, 1977.
Source: The Museum of Arts & Design, New
York. John Bigelow Taylor, photographer.

The Material Girl
to the Present

*I*n the 1980s, we felt compelled to go shopping for earrings. The jewelry in our possession, the discreet studs and fun enamel and mod plastic, looked trivial compared with what was being purveyed. I never saw *Dynasty*, the glamorous soap that became America's number one television series by 1985, but I felt its influence in the "power" jewelry at Bloomingdale's. The earrings were derivative and nothing special, but their exclusive Beverly Hills designer, Nolan Miller, did exactly what was required for Linda Evans, Joan Collins, and the other actresses playing the greedy, selfish, and oil-rich on the show. Everything, Nolan said, matched — suit, hat, gloves, and jewelry — because "when she walks down the hall, you may not know who she is, but you know she's rich, and you know you better get out the way."

Christmas was coming, my boyfriend's restaurant was on Madison Avenue, and when we strolled over on Fifth, he looked in Cartier's windows and said those earrings (I forget the stones) would suit me (I had spikey platinum hair). He was shopping for a penthouse for us that had to overlook Central Park, like the one he had with his not-quite-divorced wife, although I was ready to bail because I wasn't sure I could handle him 24/7 — but wow...I could handle getting jewelry from Cartier!

We flew in his plane to pick up some of the topiaries he always gave his wife. We made love on the garlanded balcony of his restaurant, with customers below, and then he gave me my gift — two arrowheads he had dug up himself (he stressed that) at his coastal summer property. He remarked that he'd almost bought the costly Cartier baubles, but after hearing Madonna sing "Material Girl," he gave me the arrowheads "with love" instead.

Afro-American Barbie.
Source: Mattel.

Gold and enamel
by David Webb.
Source: Brenda Ginton.

Diamond cluster.
Source: Rau Antiques.

Yellow and white diamond flowers by Oscar
Heyman.
Source: Rau Antiques.

Being "material" was more a witty fashion conceit than a way of life. It was the handy pot of a little girl's glitter that adds sparkle to whatever she creates. In the realm of jewelry, it manifested as large and flashy earrings, from the ravishing to the tasteless and balanced, high-volume hairstyles to dramatic makeup. The 1980s saw big clips designed to draw attention to the head, jagged shapes, and also discs with volume. My jewelry box simply doesn't have room for the gigantesque, though I held onto one '80s pair, after most went to little girls' dress-up: silver-white solid discs, with a gold hue buried inside and a yolk in an egg, also reminiscent of a *Star Trek* spaceship lighting up the sky. My mother expressed puzzlement when we saw them in a store — what looked beautiful to me were chunky gewgaws to her.

PRETTY WOMAN

The shop women who condescend to Vivian in *Pretty Woman* wear typical 1980s earrings: super big, hard-edged, geometrical shapes, probably hollow metal tubes. Earrings are thematic. Buccellati's emporium is right next to where Richard Gere as the tycoon and Julia Roberts the prostitute (who flosses and can drive an Alfa at top speed through L.A.) tryst. Being a good customer, he borrows from the jeweler's a sapphire necklace and earrings before flying his Cinderella to San Francisco to attend an opera. When Julia Roberts went to take out the earrings, Richard Gere snaps the case on her fingers. She laughs. It was customary for the tycoon to call down to Buccellati's and Gere is unflappable when she wears the precious earrings into a den of iniquity to say hello to her friend, also in the trade.

Entering the 21ˢᵗ Century

Earring styles continue to be sensitive to fashion and innovative, flowering in the increasingly high level of handmade jewelry and in its marketing on the Internet. For example, Etsy has thousands of choices, allowing us to shop its worldwide bazaar.

Wearing earrings continues to be about attitude as much as the objects. Muriel Brandolini, an interior decorator, likes to make rooms look like a jewel box. Her husband, Nuno Brandolini d'Adda, an Italian aristocrat and investment banker, gave her 11-carat diamond studs more than 100 years old. They were mine-cut and so had large facets and were less sparkly than today's brilliant cut stones. He handed them to her in a little box, but she knew what they were. "Of course, I knew they were diamonds!" she told a *New York Times* reporter. "He wouldn't dare give me a piece of glass!" She wears the earrings to take out the trash and go to the grocery store. "They're so big, no one thinks they are diamonds."

A jewelry trend for the stars that spotlights earrings is either/or — as opposed to full sets. On the cover of the November 2003 *Los Angeles Magazine*, Sharon Stone was stunning in a slip of a strapless dress and sparkling dangling earrings. In the November 2010 *InStyle* magazine, Jessica Alba wore a ruffled gray silk chemise by Valentino and thirty carats of yellow and white Bulgari earrings. In a 1995 photograph, Gwyneth Paltrow and her mother, Blythe Danner, are wrapped in satiny folds of evening gowns and their earrings are dainty focal points. At the 2011 Grammys, Nicole Kidman wore a strapless floral print mermaid gown by Jean Paul Gaultier, which she matched with chocolate heels and vintage Fred Leighton jewelry — an emerald and diamond encrusted gold bangle and gold and emerald earrings.

Chaumet, Winston, or Bougeron still offer formal suites to the super-rich. We like to see them on celebri-

Mismatched Triangle Studs.
Source: Caitlin Mociun.

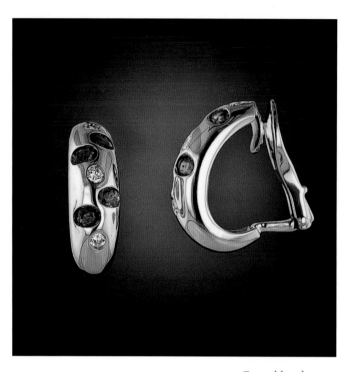

Emerald and
diamond partial
hoops.
Source: Lang Antique &
Estate Jewelry.

Swarovski dangles
(spring-summer
2000 catalog).
Source: Swarovski-U.S.

Swarovski leaves
(summer 2002 catalog).
Source: Swarovski-U.S.

ties or our Barbie dolls. It's lovely to stroll the fabled streets of European capitals or Fifth Avenue or Rodeo Drive and see luxury shops with jewelry of fabled gems and prices. Online we can compare and select with unprecedented sophistication. We still care about real versus fake. We also care about Fair Trade diamonds and gold. We treasure antique pairs of earrings without feeling a need to reset them.

After Kris Humphries tossed Kim Kardashian into the ocean on their honeymoon, she put her hand to her ear and found it bare. "My earring's gone! Oh my god, I'm going to cry!" she announced to the reality TV spectators. She was distraught from losing $175,000 of bling. Her new spouse tried to reassure her with "We'll find it baby," but she knew they were lost to the sea. Later, Kris mused for the camera that the honeymoon had just begun and his bride had already "freaked out." He wondered what was ahead...divorce, seventy-two days later. Rightly or wrongly, he just wasn't that concerned about losing the diamond earring, but one has to wonder why Kim was even wearing such costly jewelry to the beach?

Of all items of jewelry earrings continue to have a sensual sub-message. In the movie *Someone Like You* (2001), Hugh Jackman says to Ashley Judd, "Here, you left these earrings in my bathroom" to be suggestive and tease her in front of co-workers at the television station. In "Tequila Makes Her Clothes Fall Off," Joe Nichols sings, "She'll start by kicking off her shoes/ Lose an earring in her drink/ Leave her jacket in the bathroom stall/ Drop a contact down the sink." Then the next morning she says, "Oh, what have I done?"

Martin Katz, whose celebrity clients include Jennifer Aniston, Selma Hayek, Angelina Jolie, Kate

Blanchett, Kate Winslet, Heidi Klum, and Anne Heche, does "contemporary pieces for an old soul," infusing vintage and classic styles with a modern edge. Caitlin Mociun's unmatched studs have subtle charm, not the '80s kind of kick. Feathers enter many designs; they say, "I'm light and lovely on the planet." Huggies draw attention to the curve of the ear and cheek and shoulder-dusters show off the athleticism of arms and shoulders. Diversity is in.

Former Olympic swimmer Charlene Wittstock of South Africa became a princess when she married Prince Albert II of Monaco in 2011 in a civil ceremony at the prince's palace followed by a second ceremony in a church. At the first, she wore a blue Chanel jacket over palazzo pants and accessorized the ensemble with a pair of diamond earring studs. At the church ceremony, she shed the earrings and all the jewelry holding back her hair. The message was that this was low-key — and proper. The latter-day princess wears striking arabesque, squiggle, and other fashionable designer earrings that point up she's smart, athletic, and fashionable. Chandelier earrings and large pendants with dramatic strapless gowns might have been worn by Princess Grace — the more valuable the stones in an earring today, the more predictable and nearly dateless the styles.

More than ever jewelry is individualistic with no style dominant. The divide is more who wears machine-made and likes to grab a pair at the drugstore to go with a mood or dress while others shop for what is handcrafted and unique. We are looking for meaning in the luxuries our civilization has wrought. This is apparent in how international gem and jewelry expert and author Antoinette Matlins answers, "What is your favorite pair?"

Bridal and ear cuffs.
Source: SusanThierriere-Henry.

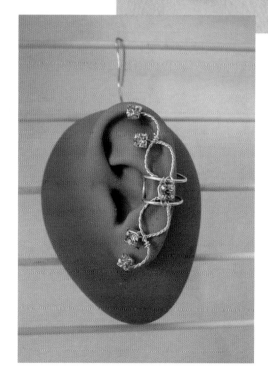

My favorite pair are simple studs, each comprised of a large, round, natural pearl (that is, not cultured). Throughout history, natural pearls have been regarded as the most precious of all gems. The large pearls in these earrings — almost 11 millimeters in diameter — are lustrous, white saltwater pearls that most likely originated from the Persian Gulf at least over a century ago. My engagement ring is a natural pearl too, from the mid-1800s, with an exquisitely lustrous natural pearl at the center, an antique-cut diamond flanking each side.

MICHELLE OBAMA

Few will become hot under the collar over whether Ralph Lauren, Giorgio Armani, Brooks Brothers, or a tailor in Hong Kong made the suits worn by the President of the United States, but the First Lady's ensembles are very much in the public eye. Michelle Obama is seen mostly in American-made earrings at public occasions. Her earrings receive nearly as much press as her gowns, and this is without precedent. Mrs. Obama coordinates her earrings with her outfit, rather than selecting them from sentiment or to impress. The moonstone and diamond drops went with the whole pink tint of her ensemble, down to her rhubarb pumps. Chandeliers with glass pearls had a Spanish look for a visit to El Salvador. A strapless gown by an Indian-American designer was accessorized for a state dinner honoring the Indian prime minister with pear-shaped pendants with amber and tourmalines, suspended from gold fleur-de-lys. To dine at Buckingham Palace, she wore a halter neck white ivory Tom Ford gown with shoulder length pale bluish green crystal teardrops. Most are in the range of costume jewelry although the amazonite double ovals framed with rubies by Phillips Frankel of New York, which she wore after Obama's election for a second term, cost several thousand dollars.

Tall and statuesque, with beautiful hair and skin, sparkling eyes and smile, Michelle has chosen to make her jewelry statement predominately with her earrings. They have a dramatic effect...they — and not a necklace or bracelet — are *de rigueur*, and, as we've seen over time, they also are often friendly diplomatic gestures. The earrings not only coordinate with her clothes, but the tenor of the public occasion. It was okay to wear trendy large rose gold sapphire-studded hoops to the White House Correspondents Association Dinner, but perhaps not to a state dinner. In 2012, ruby and geode earrings were her choice at a banquet for the Chinese president, wearing them with a sumptuous Alexander McQueen petal print red and black full-length gown. These were by jewelry designer Kimberly McDonald, who didn't learn Michelle was going to wear her earrings to the state dinner until a friend texted her, "Are those yours?"... Bonanza!

We can imagine that this First Lady often has earrings on her mind as she prepares for her day, and having them in mind led once to a gaffe during Obama's first presidential campaign. This happened in the context of a quip about tax stimulus. On July 9, 2008, Mrs. Obama said at a rally in Pontiac, Michigan, that if elected her husband would offer more to the economy than his opponents, as follows:

You're getting $600 — what can you do with that?... The short-term quick fix kinda stuff sounds good, and it may even feel good that first month when you get that check, and then you go out and you buy a pair of earrings.

Earrings figured more positively during the second campaign when singer Beyonce showed her support for President Obama by dining out with her husband Jay-Z in New York wearing gold hoops with the word Obama spelled out: the hoop made the "O", with a "BAMA" charm dangling from the top. Designer Erika Pena sold these instantly collectible baubles in silver and gold for 32 dollars.

Green eyes.
Source: Margaux Lange.

BARBIE GOES BURLESQUE

Fashion dolls circulated what the proper courtier wore in 1700, but later the fashions migrated from adult styles to dolls. Thus, the '80s over-the-top assertion of feminine glamour lived on in the Barbie dolls of the Nineties, when my youngest daughter, Rosalind, and I would go to the toy store as an outing. We window shopped the resplendent new looks from Mattel, some of which on the Collectible Barbies were by Bob Mackie, a top designer for performers like Cher. The Barbies in the most lavish gowns had two accessories we extolled — the little plastic shoes and the silver- or gold-toned jewelry. The Barbies, in their pendants, hoops, and cascades, are the last word of dress-up, and my daughter imagined wonderful narratives and scenes with her Barbies without desiring to be a stick-like blonde. The earrings on a lavish Barbie stand out from her metallic or satin outfit, fake fur and lace. Take off the earrings and you lose the whole showgirl thing that, in the '80s, when glitz maxed out, had my friends and me tromping around in silver and gold strappy platform shoes, glittering leggings, earrings as big as lollipops, and so forth. We were declaring a sense of our own beauty, and fundamentally Barbie, like any doll, **serves** for being whatever you wish, in the alternative world of play.

Should dolls be re-purposed into jewelry? The answer is, if done well, yes. The artist Margaux Lange salvages pre-owned Barbies and using the mass-produced parts creates handmade jewelry — wearable art. The doll eye or ear, set in sterling with pigmented resin epoxy (preserving it as in in amber), juxtaposes with the person's ears and eyes. Observes Lange, "Barbie has become the accessory instead of being accessorized." My daughters and I wouldn't wear the "leg" necklaces — they remind me of a neighbor's standard poodle who ate the plastic dolls it found around the house — but we would like to wear the blue eyes or doll smile. Given the plethora of the jewelry for sale, it's a pleasure to gravitate to new earring art.

Blossoms.
Source: Margaux Lange.

Black drops with blue eye shadow.
Source: Margaux Lange.

Cutting Gems to be Used as Earrings

by Rafai Swiecki, Geological Engineer

Author's Note: Tradition, crystallography and aesthetics govern how gems are cut. This Canadian geological engineer and multilingual expert in alluvial exploration and mining projects gives us some rudiments — cutting through an unfathomable complexity of his field.

The modes of cutting in vogue at the present day are the results of centuries of trial and observation on the part of gem-cutters. The form in which transparent stones are cut differs from that best suited to opaque stones; and in the same way, the form in which dark-colored stones are cut differs from that given to lighter or colorless stones.

The amount of refraction and dispersion exercised upon light by a transparent stone greatly affects its appearance. To obtain a maximum effect, the greater part of the light, which enters by the front facets of a cut stone, must be reflected from the back facets and pass out again by the front facets. Since the path of a ray of light in a stone varies with the refractive index of the specific mineral, the form of cutting must be adapted to each mineral.

Importantly, the number and arrangements of the facets differ, but each was designed to give the best presentation of the mineral's color and transparency with minimum loss from the original crystal.

Cabochon or rounded, the most ancient form, has the stone polished and unfaceted. Now as a general rule, only transparent stones are faceted; chalcedony and other translucent stones are occasionally cut in this way; opaque stones, like turquoise, moonstone, carnelian, amber, star sapphire or star ruby, always are cut en cabochon.

Rose or rosette has the facets all on one side, the other side being occupied by a single large face. When such a stone is set as a jewel, the side turned towards the observer is known as the upper portion or crown, while the opposite side or lower portion is referred to as the culasse or pavilion. The whole forms a double pyramid with truncated summits, each pyramid having a common base in the girdle. The appearance has been compared to the opening of a rosebud. It has been in vogue since about 1530, principally for diamonds of small thickness, from which comparatively small brilliants only could be obtained. The rose cut displays the brilliance of the stone well, and is also applied to colored stones such as garnets, amethysts, aquamarines, or other transparent colored semi-precious gems.

The brilliant form of cutting was first used by Cardinal Mazarin to revive the diamond-cutting industry in Paris. The superiority of the brilliant over all other forms of cutting for diamonds and other colorless, transparent stones, and also for some colored stones is now so firmly established that it is at present by far the most generally used. Indeed, for this reason diamonds are often referred to colloquially as "brilliants." Colored transparent stones are very frequently brilliant cut but not so invariably as with diamonds. Ideally in a brilliant the height of the upper portion above the girdle is one-third of the total thickness of the stone from table to culet and the diameters of the table and culet are respectively five-ninths and one-ninth of the diameter of the girdle; hence the diameter of the table is five times that of the culet. (The girdle of a brilliant is sometimes left with sharp edges, as is the custom of English gem-cutters, or the edges may be ground down, as is done in Holland, to prevent chipping).

Several varieties of the brilliant-cut are distinguished according to the number of facets.

For larger stones the triple-cut brilliant is most appropriate. Here three series of facets lie one above the other on the upper part of the stone; the total of thirty-two facets, exclusive of the table, is made up of eight triangular star facets, sixteen triangular cross facets, and eight four-sided facets.

The half-brilliant (or brillionette) has a single large face on the underside, which forms a base to the upper portion as in rosettes.

Parisian jeweler Caire, which had its establishment at the Place de Vendome at the beginning of the 19th century, devised the star-cut, which is closely related to the brilliant form. In this form the facets are arranged in multiples of six, and the gemstone has a star-like appearance.

The step or trapiche cut has step-like facets of the upper portion. The cut is square, rectangular or hexagonal and has facets that are rectilinear and arranged parallel to the girdle. Popular in the Art Deco period, it includes types like lozenge, baguette, and trapezoid.

Table-cut includes a number of forms related to a four-sided double pyramid joined by bases or regular octahedron. This octahedral form is the natural crystalline form of diamonds best suited for brilliant cut, since one crystal, with minimum loss of material, can be cut into two equal or one larger and other smaller faceted gems. It may sometimes be seen in the jewelry that dates back to the time when no cutting of the rough stones was attempted, but the preparation of the stones for ornamental purposes was confined to polishing the natural faces of the crystals. To derive the table-cut from the octahedron involves truncating two opposite corners; a few additional facets may be given to the upper portion of the stone.

Next are the briolettes or pendeloques, which are bounded by small facets on all sides, and are somewhat elongated in one direction, so they have a pear-shaped outline. They are often pierced in the direction of their greatest length so as to be used as earrings.

The Koh-i-noor, which means "Mountain of Light," was taken (stolen) as part of the Treaty of Lahore from Punjab when it was incorporated into the British India. It was cut from 186.05 carats to its current 105.60 carats to increase its brilliance, to be offered to Queen Victoria. Its oval shape departs from the typical round brilliant form.

The Regent, originally a 410-carats stone, was cut to become a 136.87-carats brilliant. Now part of the French crown jewels, the Regent is perhaps the most perfectly beautiful stone of its kind existing at the present day. It conforms with the greatest precision to the proportions laid down for the brilliant, and consequently far surpasses the Koh-i-noor in brilliancy and play of colors, although the two stones are equal in quality.

Insofar as dressing up the ears goes with flirtation and the evening, a stone with a special allure for earrings is alexandrite due to its mysterious color change, from green in daylight to shades of red under artificial light at night, which you can actually see happen (a blaze of color) in a low lit room. Originally discovered in Russia in 1834 and used in Victorian times by jewelers like Tiffany, there was a further discovery of fine alexandrites in Brazil in 1984. The stones are also lab-made, like the one in the picture. A natural alexandrite, over five carats, costs more than diamond or ruby of the same size.

Studs Who Wear Them

> " *It seems she hangs on the cheek of night
> Like a rich jewel in an Ethiop's ear.* "
>
> ~ William Shakespeare, *Romeo and Juliet*

hile we were married, Chris wore a wedding band and used a woodsy cologne he ordered from New Orleans. That was the sum of his adornment: no other jewelry or interest in my purchases of antique earrings. After our divorce, he remarried, and his new wife bought him a gold chain that he removes only for a massage or MRI. He took a new job in North Carolina, and his wife stayed behind in Alexandria, Virginia, to sell their house and pack their belongings. While temporarily alone in Raleigh, he bought onyx studs in a shopping mall corridor, where a young woman also pierced his left earlobe — and sent him on to the rest of his life. Somewhat changed, he declared, but to what?

Like many men, my co-author does not relate much to his feelings. They're there all right but largely hidden to the owner. As we started researching this book, I challenged him to a span of retro- and intro-spection. He went back to our late 1960s wedding. Sure that the Beatles and Nehru jackets would endure forever, he came to the altar in an Indian pundit's collarless shirt and ecru Nehru jacket. Not so unconventional were his bellbottom twill pants. He wanted to be different but not radically, the same as with the earring. At North Carolina State University, he wanted to stand out from the engineers, not by a hoop or shiny stone, but just a small black stud in one ear. Chris says his jewelry fling hinted at the rogue "safely inside," and was maybe modeled after popular culture heroes who also wore a stud. The latter he has forgotten as we all have but the earring endures.

Ashurnasiripal II (883–859 BC), the Assyrian king, is well known to us because he rebuilt a great city, Nimrud, on the banks of the Tigris River. The walls of his palace were lined with carved gypsum showing many images of the king and descriptions of his military and political exploits. The reliefs depict the king's strong physique in his arms and legs, visible in the cuts of his long robe and

Ashurnasiripal II.
Source: Erich Lessing Art Resource, New York.

sandals. He sports a square beard in stylized curls, a fez-like crown, long hair tied with a band which trails down his back, and earrings of power. A hoop pierces the earlobe and a pendant of gold hangs two inches down. In the reliefs, the king's attendants, most likely eunuchs, and divine winged helpers also wear earrings, as do the enormous human-headed lions that guard the doors of the palace. The earrings are fully masculine — prominent and simple — and their appearance on attendants and genies as well as the king indicates that they were *de rigueur* for men in the royal court. To approach the great king, males donned their earrings.

Starting from a territory in what is today northern Iraq, Ashurnasiripal expanded Assyrian rule east to the Iranian border and west to the Mediterranean Sea. The western move would bring the Assyrians into the Old Testament a century later when the Assyrian conquerors defeated Israel, ending the rule of Jewish kings and scattering the Jewish population throughout the Near East, the so-called lost tribes. Hebrew prophets such as Hosea and Isaiah saw this as God's punishment for the Israelites' lax obedience to God's commandments and forever set in the Western religious mind the idea that God acts through worldly events however destructive they may be.

Ashurnasiripal rebuilt on the banks of the upper Tigris River a small city, originally known as Kalhu but later and more famously as Nimrud, into a great imperial center. A great administrator as well as conqueror, Ashurnasiripal brought to the capital both captives to work on construction crews and an immense booty of gold and precious stones to stock his treasury. A cuneiform inscription on the walls of his palace declares:

I am Ashurnasiripal, the obedient prince, the worshiper of the Great Gods, the fierce dragon, the conqueror of all cities and mountains to their full extent, the king of rulers, who tames the dangerous enemies, the (one) crowned with glory, the

(one) unafraid of battle, the relentless lion, who shakes resistance, the king (deserving) of praise, the shepherd, protector of the world, the king whose command blots out mountains and seas, who forced into compliance the relentless, fierce kings from the East to the West, at his very approach.

Ashurnasiripal was so dominant that once his borders were stable he invited thousands of dignitaries from all over his newly expanded territory for a great feast, but empires come and go — and the Assyrians fell to the Persians. Nimrud and its great palace fell into ruin and remained a large mound, or tell, until the 1840s when a young Englishman without much purpose happened on the large tell, which covered the ancient city.

Henry Layard was traveling across Iraq toward faraway Ceylon (present day Sri Lanka) to find employment there in the British civil service. On a stopover in Mosul, he happened upon the great ruins of Nimrud, where he spent the next six years excavating and removing many tons of reliefs and statues to the British Museum. In Nimrud and other near Eastern sites, such as Babylon and Nineveh, Layard found a lot of ancient jewelry. Most of the pieces he sent to museums, but he kept select items for himself. In 1869, he had the English jeweler Phillips transform a set of cameos into a necklace and earrings for his wife, Mary.

From Ashurnasiripal, an Olympic hop, skip, and jump over the classical Greeks and Romans, takes us to the Byzantine Empire, which flourished from the fourth to the fifteenth century. In the Byzantine East, personal adornment survived the conversion of Constantine to the Christian faith and flourished in the court. While the western part, including Rome, had suffered the ravages of the Goths and other marauding tribes, the eastern part, anchored in Constantinople, flourished. Emperor Justinian actually conquered and rebuilt Rome, sponsored a major revision of Roman law, rebuilt the Hagia

Emperor Justinian I (c. 547 AD).
Source: San Vitale, Ravenna, Italy,
Bridgeman Art Library.

A century before Justinian, Augustine, the bishop of Hippo in North Africa and the most influential Christian of his day, criticized some Christian women for wearing their hair uncovered, and for painting their faces "to make themselves more pink and white," and some young men for wearing earrings "on the top part of the ear, hanging down one side." These the bishop attacked as amulets left over from a pagan past. We conclude that yes, some men wore earrings, and yes, as the church grew stronger in Western Europe, women would cover their hair and ears and men would discard ear decoration altogether. The Byzantine love of earrings would continue among the tribal invaders such as the Franks and Ostrogoths who gradually brought down the Romans (see Chapter 2, page 12), but only among women.

A long jump over the Middle Ages takes us to the 1500s when some men again donned earrings. In England, the Tudors came to power in 1485 when Henry VII took power, ending the long War of the Roses. There is no evidence that this Henry's courtiers wore earrings, but a portrait of his son, Henry VIII, shows a pearl drop in one ear. Henry's was a lavish if troubled court — "divorced, beheaded, died, divorced, beheaded, survived" denotes the fates of his six wives — and gold and pearls were plentiful. Henry was a Renaissance king in that he composed music — perhaps "Greensleeves" so familiar to us — spoke and read Latin and French as fluently as his native English, wrote a religious treatise, danced with grace, and loved a good party. The earring was a mark of his culture rather than of his rule.

In the court of Henry's daughter, Elizabeth I, several courtiers and the world's most famous playwright continued Henry's fashion. Most notable among the earringed courtiers were the queen's dashing sea-faring adventurers Francis Drake and Walter Raleigh. Both wore single earrings in the left ear. Drake was a privateer of the first water. Loyal to the queen, he ran down Spanish galleons en route from the Caribbean to Spain loaded with silver and gold — alas, they did not bring

Sophia, and put in place roads and walls and other infrastructure that kept Constantinople flourishing and safe until the thirteenth century. Like his wife, Theodora, Emperor Justinian (ruled 527–565) wore striking earrings on both ears. Mosaics usually show the emperor with two single pearls on each ear, one on a wire attached to the upper ear and one attached to the lobe. Unlike the solid discs Ashurnasiripal wore, Justinian's earrings are fey, angling out from his neck as though blowing in the wind. Though smaller and less colorful than the gorgeous earrings gracing the ears of his empress, Theodora, they hang in marked contrast to the increasingly denuded ears of the western empire.

back platinum, which was too hard to work with wood or coal fires. To the queen went half the spoils, to Drake and his crew the other half. During most of his career, the English and Spanish were not at war, so to the Spanish, Drake was really a pirate, in their terms a "dragon." Although the Spanish vowed to capture "this pirate, this heretic, blind in his greed...like a fish with the hook in its gills," the English defeat of the Spanish Armada in 1588 forever deflated Spanish revenge. A key figure in the sea battle of 1588, Drake continued his sea adventures even though he was wealthy, and he died far from home of dysentery and was buried in a lead coffin off the coast of Nicaragua. To this day, divers scour the sea floor in search of the great seaman.

Walter Raleigh was also a child of the Age of Discovery and seafaring fellow to Drake. He was a wealthy landowner commissioned by Queen Elizabeth to found a colony in the New World. More the entrepreneur than Drake, Raleigh sent a group of men and women to settle in Roanoke. Though the colony vanished from neglect, the effort endeared him to the queen and gave him a prominent place in America's history. He was a bit of a rogue: when he married one of the queen's ladies-in-waiting without the monarch's permission, Elizabeth sent him to the Tower — but on the whole the queen favored him, knighted him, and made him wealthy. Like Drake he sailed to the Spanish Main in search of gold and silver. He explored the coasts of Venezuela and Guiana in search of a fabled city paved with gold and studded with precious jewels. His reports did much to establish El Dorado as a real though hidden city worthy of the full efforts of England's finest explorers to discover. Although he lacked Drake's prowess and reputation as a raider of Spanish ships and colonies, Raleigh did his share of killing and burning in his search for wealth. Queen Elizabeth's successor, James I, viewed the popular Raleigh with suspicion and even sentenced him to death for participating in a conspiracy to overthrow the king. Evidence was skimpy and the king released

Raleigh, but, in a subsequent raid on the Spanish colony San Tome de Guyana, Raleigh left few survivors. England and Spain were technically at peace and the Spanish ambassador pressed James to reinstate the death penalty that he had previously rescinded. Raleigh was beheaded, but lives on as one of England's most esteemed heroes.

Shakespeare circulated in Elizabeth's court as playwright and actor. In the portrait printed in the first folio of his plays, his ears are undecked, but in another, known as the Chandos portrait, a shiny gold hoop dangles from his left ear. The earring was perhaps a bit dandyish, perhaps a bit bohemian, and in all cases a statement by a manly wearer. What about gender? On the Elizabethan stage, men played women's roles, causing us moderns to rapidly shift our categories as we think of the Shakespearean women who disguised themselves as men: men playing women pretending to be men. Several of his plays feature women disguised as men — for example, Viola in *Twelfth Night*, Portia in *The Merchant of Venice*, and Rosalind (my daughter's namesake) in *As You Like It*. In *The Merry Wives of Windsor* and *The Taming of the Shrew*, men disguise themselves as women, an easier convention. To Shakespeare's audiences, moving from gender to gender provided a playful background to the adventurers and courtiers who wore earrings but remained clearly masculine.

Like Raleigh, whom Nils Sture must have met on a diplomatic mission to the court of Queen Elizabeth, the Swedish aristocrat wore a single earring for formal occasions and, like Raleigh, he fell under the shadow of his monarch's suspicion of treason. In the 1560s, Sweden's king, Eric XIV, grew increasingly suspicious of the nobles who owned most of the land and dominated the king's privy council. Among the nobles, he feared the Sture family the most, especially Svante Sture and his son Nils. Eric executed the father for treason, but commuted Nils's sentence to a humiliating ride through Stockholm in a rickety carriage, wearing a straw crown.

Leonard Limosin, *Francis II as Dauphin of France* (c. 1560).
Source: Louvre, Paris, Bridgeman Art Library.

Jean Decourt, *Henry III, King of France* (c. 1581).
Source: RMN-Grand Palais, Art Resource, New York

William Shakespeare (Chandos Portrait).
Source: National Portrait Gallery, London.

Nils reconciled with Eric, who sent him on a diplomatic mission to Lorraine, but the king's suspicions verged into madness and upon Nils's return to Sweden, he was arrested for treason. While awaiting trial, the king visited Nils's cell and personally stabbed him to death. The king then left his royal quarters and wandered the countryside in a peasant's disguise until he was discovered and formally deposed.

Though they worked for the queen, Drake and Raleigh do link with a long tradition of piracy, to the general lawlessness of the open seas. Even the strongest governments had trouble with pirates because the sea is vast and the ships few. Pirates, at least successful

Nils Sture.
Source: Swedish National
Museum

Angelica
Kauffmann,
Chevalier
D'Eon (1788),
18th-Century
French cross-
dresser.
Source: Private
Collection,
Bridgeman Art
Library.

pirates, were famous for dressing up after a lucra-
tive capture. Several captured pilots recounted how
victorious pirates rifled clothes chests and jewelry and
paraded about in their newfound finery to celebrate
their catch. Jewelry seems to fit this tradition, an early
form of bling flaunted by the outsider, a kind of one-
upsmanship. One popular tradition has it that sailors
wore earrings valuable enough to pay for a proper
burial in case the wearer drowned and washed ashore,
but historical evidence for this is scarce. The popular
image of the pirate wearing baggy pants, a tricorn hat,
showy belts and bandoleers, and gold hoop earrings
can be traced to the early twentieth century and the
illustrations of Howard Pyle. In his popular *Book of
Pirates* (1921), Pyle, a Quaker but long time aficionado
of pirates, showed the buccaneer Henry Morgan wearing gold hoops. In *The Black Pirate* (1926), Douglas
Fairbanks sported sizable gold hoops; thus, in the
popular mind, earrings became associated with seafaring thieves.

Across the English Channel in France, cross-
dressing moved from the theater to the court itself.
François-Timoleon, Abbé de Choisy, was born in 1644,
a late birth to a popular courtier at Versailles who had
a weekly tête-à-tête with Louis XIV. Happy to have
borne a child in her middle age, she decided to raise
this third son as a girl. His ears were pierced and he
wore beauty marks, patches that came in different
sizes and shapes and were high style on white-pow-
dered faces in mid-seventeenth century France. Daily
he applied a depilatory to his face. In adult life, De
Choisy had an extraordinary transvestite existence.
He liked to have people guessing, as when he was
five months on the stage in Bordeaux disguised as a
woman. He wrote books of gossip and history, as well
as a romance where the shepherd dressed as a woman.
After a grave illness, he became devout and accompanied French missionaries on a trip to Siam. De Choisy
was well-matched with his times. Like the English,

the French celebrated gender role switches, whether to insinuate a lover in *The Marriage of Figaro* or to dance with whomever at masked balls.

The King's brother Philippe, "Monsieur," the duc d'Orléans, four years older than the Abbé de Choisy, was a cross-dresser. Philippe, born in 1644 as the second son of Anne of Austria and Louis XII, was raised by women as a girl. Abbé de Choisy's mother taught her son to curtsy and took him to visit her friend Clélie several times a week in a concerted effort to feminize him. Philippe went everywhere with his mother, powdered, and covered in flounces. Surprisingly, Philippe found an occupation as a military man, and was considered an estimable general, but Louis obliged him to return to Versailles with the courtiers upon whom the king kept a close eye. Philippe was a passionate collector of porcelain and rare objects, especially gems. At his death he was in possession of two big single diamonds, three hundred parures of diamonds, one hundred of pearls, fifty of emeralds, and many of sapphires and rubies.

De Choisy too collected gems and jewelry. In a memoir, he writes of smaller earrings for at-home wear and larger ones for parties, smaller ones for bedtime (to keep the piercings) and earrings of diamonds, rubies and emeralds to look gorgeous for balls and *fêtes*. He may have dropped a girl he had seduced for getting pregnant, but he never failed to give a former sweetheart a pair of earrings. He gave one well-bred but provincial inamorata a pair as a token of their bed sport, but kept the gift modest so that the mother wouldn't suspect he and the girl were

having sex. When they wed, he felt free to give her a much more valuable pair as a present. In his forties, his romantic life waned, but this, he wrote, increased his love of earrings. Even as he took on the celibate life of a clergyman, he continued to crossdress.

Howard Pyle, *Book of Pirates* (New York: Harper & Bros., 1921). Source: Stony Brook University Libraries.

THE BUCCANEER WAS A PICTURESQUE FELLOW

Contemporary Art

> " *Ornament implies that decorative fors are alive, that they breathe more easily than ponderous statues and endless Madonnas.* "

~ Oleg Grabar, *The Mediation of Ornament*

Source: Rachel Adams.

he jewelers selected for this chapter's contemporary showcase share the qualities of originality, artistic and technical accomplishment, and unique understanding of the place of earrings in the field of adornment. Instead of trying, as U2 sings, to throw our arms around the world, I honor the diversity of earrings in (mostly) the U.S. Like a stargazer, I have scanned the sky for most intriguing, diverse, and praiseworthy pairs.

My step-daughter, Alina, was wearing attractive earrings with the silver mark of Gorham, made from spoons, which she bought at a crafts fair, that led me to steampunk. An online image of ravishing and elite chandeliers led me to fine French-American jewelers. I wanted computer-aided design and found an expert at work in a room of the Providence Museum. Another designer represents museum-quality work in an atypical metal, titanium. One designer sells directly on the streets of New York and another does a hot California look. In summer, I don earbobs of red gold paper, and in the form of bowed turquoise plastic high-heels, so I looked for museum exhibitions of origami, and on Etsy for the most excellent miniatures. I sought a silversmith, a beader, and a native American who creates with quills; and, from writing about love relationships, recalled earrings that show sexual arousal, and its inventors shared information about this innovation here.

Rachael Victoria Adams

– Southern California

Rachel Adams turns vintage findings into exceptional jewelry. She uses the steampunk art form where technology is modified to create objects of surprise.

In my studio, Nouveau Motley, I upcycle components and relics of natural history to build jewelry which is meticulous. Many pieces feature found objects from the Victorian and Art Deco periods repurposed into wearable works of art. Often I combine antique clockworks with genuine skulls and beetles. I believe I instill an air of bio-mechanical memento mori into the jewelry I create.

Findings I usually incorporate are Victorian pocket watch parts, Victorian and Art Deco buttons, Art Deco beads, and pieces of broken antique jewelry (usually sections of rhinestone bracelets or necklaces dating to the art deco/retro periods).

I view the process as creative problem-solving. I have thousands of antique, vintage and modern components, and my work comes out of a sort of creative chaos. I have an idea of the shape or design in mind and then find what fits to bring that idea into fruition.

I have an online store only, but also vend at art and craft shows.

Janet Deleuse, jewelry designer

– San Francisco, California

I'm a California girl. I met my husband at age twenty-two and his family became mine. His father is from Nice, mother from Vienna — they speak French, German, Spanish, and English all intermingled. I think we have our own language sometimes. We have family in Nice and Antibes, whom we visit often, and I feel as if I'm European. Our store continues the European tradition of jewelers; all of our jewelry is high-end, either made by us or from Germany, Italy, and France.

Designing one-off earrings is my specialty! I created one-off clothes from age 12 and just morphed into jewelry. I was a science major in college, molecular biology. We mix our gold and hand-fabricate. Most of my inspirations are from what young hip girls wear on the streets — that's what makes fashion. We travel the world. A pair of earrings I call "Bohemian Earrings" (see opposite page) are inspired from the streets of Paris in July 2011, because that summer Parisian women were going back to the 1960s in peasant blouses, long skirts, and dangling jewelry — very natural, I loved the change. The earrings are hand-fabricated in 18-carat white gold with pavé-set, round, brilliant perfect diamonds, surrounding natural aquamarines and peridots (cut in Idar-Oberstein for me) with sapphire briolettes dangling. I usually use platinum for a white metal, but it is grayer in tone than the white gold we mix and plate with rhodium, that I chose to use for this pair.

A JEWELRY DESIGNER ON STYLE

More than any other item a person wears — it's the earrings, at a glance that will convey personality, style and a statement to the world. From olden times to today, earrings deliver a message, which the wearer transmits instantly without uttering a word. Whether it is a message of prosperity or simplicity, chic or eccentricity, historically or culturally significant, the communication is clear.

The ancient Persian Kings and Indian Maharajas wore large natural pearls in their ears to express their extreme wealth and supremacy — and command respect. In ancient times, natural pearls were the most valuable of all gems.

Cleopatra conquered her opponent, the Roman Commander, Marc Antony, without combat, when she seduced him by betting that she could "give him the most expensive meal he'll ever have" and won, by causally dropping one of her large, natural oriental pearls in his wine, offering it to him to drink after it dissolved. She not only won her battle, she won his heart — what could have better commanded respect? In comparison, today's musicians wear huge, lightning-bolt dazzling diamonds in both ears, gaining respect and awe from their devoted wannabe fans.

During ceremonial occasions, sentimental earrings are, almost always, part of the costume. Brides traditionally wear earrings worn by their mothers and mothers before them. Ancient ritualistic performances adorn dancers with old-styled jewelry — jingling earrings in shapes of chimeras, bells and reflective colors.

Earrings are a cultural symbol — travel the world to Africa, Asia, Europe, and the Americas and find the most bizarre to the blandest. Identifiable to a particular culture, the design can remain the same to that culture throughout centuries. The number and size of piercings are symbolic for Amazon Indians and the Massai Africans. They wear multiple large, intricately beaded earrings intertwined with several strands wrapped around their necks, chests, and forearms — so integral to their bodies, it's almost impossible to see each jewel individually. I own hand-wired steel/plastic beaded Massai earrings that are better in workmanship/style than some earring repairs I take from customers — Tiffany's, worth thousands — not considering materials.

Indians wear the golden, brassy glow of pure gold earrings, which connect from their ears to their noses decorated with striking, reflective colorful emeralds,

Deep purple.
Source: Janet Deleuse.

"Bohemian Earrings" – aquamarines, peridots, diamonds with sapphire briolettes.
Source: Janet Deleuse.

rubies, sapphires and diamonds set against their flawless, dark-toned skin. Long, dangling clusters of small gold balls, with golden droplets of tiny pure gold beads attached, the Balinese dancers' earrings are essential to the precise movements of their dance, the jingling delicate tone in sync. Traditionally, Chinese women only wear pure gold and prefer the luck of the verdant gemstone jade contrasting vividly against their jet-black hair. Japanese geishas dance eloquently in earrings resembling long delicate wisteria blossoms that move, projecting sensuality, for the viewer's pleasure. Gypsy women pierce their newborn girl's ears, and as they age, their large hoop earrings or multiple rings of small stones, like a large lit chandelier, represent their unique cultural style — essential to their movements, keeping rhythm with whirling dancing. The sharp clinking of the flamenco dancer's earrings is as powerful as the distinct movements and sounds of precision clicking heels. European and Americans, in demonstrating their civility, have sometimes worn earrings that clip on, and not pierce their ears. In contrast, the Native American women and men traditionally have worn heavy, handwrought silver earrings featuring colorful turquoise and coral.

Western fashion trends dictate styles of earrings. For example, Yves Saint Laurent drew jewelry in his sketches, linear or oversized rounds, to match his seasonal runway collection. Earrings are more than an accessory; never changed or changed daily, they set the wearer's mood. The choice to be chic or counter-cultural is made clear in the selection. Audrey Hepburn wore simple pearl earrings with her modest black dress in the movie *Breakfast at Tiffany's*. She appeared unpretentious and suggestive, triggering a trend sweeping across the United States and Europe — women of all ages copied her classic, unassuming style.

Whether long dangling or modestly small, earrings should enhance the beauty of a face. The color of the precious metal, either warm golden or cool silver, and the stones should accentuate the complexion and eye color. An earring should reflect a personality and style.

I love creating earrings. Opposed to any other jewelry, there are so many options for earrings. A single pearl drop, dangling seductively, worn with a lacy camisole; large clusters of colorful gems clipped on the ear as a fashion statement; a cascade of monochromatic gems worn with a long velvet matching gown — the possibilities and need for many different earrings are endless. A single gemstone with a vibrant clarity that stirs the emotions, a perfectly formed seashell, textured wood, fruit, and fabrics, contrasting colors of leaves and flowers, an art piece — whether a simple Mondrian or complicated Dutch master: all are inspirational for me. To create and design is my reasoning and thought. In the words of philosophers and in poetry and music, I see a dimension that abstractly can be captured into something tangible — tangible to the wearer — that is the joy of my work. So, the next time you put on your favorite earrings and step out, think about your message...your individuality!

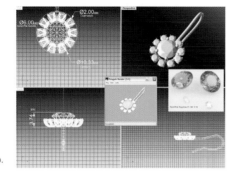

Escano sampler, one.
Source: Juan Escano Studio.

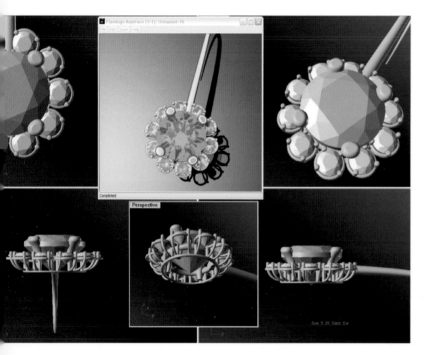

Escano sampler, two.
Source: Juan Escano Studio.

Verso.
Source: Juan Escano Studio.

Juan Escano

– Providence, Rhode Island

Juan Escano uses every technique in the book, from the lost wax process to CAD and electroform. If you lose a precious earring, he can make its exact pair in just days. He is an unstoppable talent and genie.

Here at Studio 3 we strive to discover ways of combining hundreds of years of old historical manufacturing methods with New Age technologies to create, restore, and reproduce beautiful jewelry creations. We offer everything from your traditional jeweler hand-molding to CAD customization, scanning, reverse engineering, 3-D printing, rapid prototyping, mold-making and manufacturing.

My whole life I've been self-driven. I believe if you work hard, opportunities come to you. I was forced into the jewelry industry. My sweetheart became pregnant, and I decided I had to get a job and take care of the newborn. Peter de C. was kind enough to bring me in. I began as a temp and six months later was offered a full-time position. Peter told me he wanted me to run the ring department; at seventeen, I had a lot of responsibility and by the time I was twenty-six, I was head of a department, running machines for Tiffany's, with thirty people under me and working long hours. Sometimes I worked twenty-four hours straight. I had no college education and was producing millions of dollars of jewelry a month. Now I have my own business. I love what I do; it fuels me. When I see a smile on a customer or tell my wife something I accomplished that day, it keeps me going.

Jewelry manufacture was completely different from today. The technology has taken off, derivative from computer developments for other uses such as automotive, medical and space. When I started, Peter showed me the old technology, like lost wax casting and making metal master models. First, I learned the history and then, being a young kid, the new technology caught my

attention, that I could be a designer in a matter of hours, whereas back in the day you had to study sketching and handling metal first. Yet the history of jewelry of past centuries is still close to my heart. A lot of times I am involved with a model but ask, "Is it manufacture-able?" Sometimes I hit the floor and find models in this massive building and see how a similar piece was made. For instance, it can't be cast, but needs tooling. I streamline my design; I work out the kinks so when it hits the floor the engineers can run with it, instead of weeks of dialogue to create a model.

A customer comes to me with one earring and wants the mate, and the only way to bring it back is 3-D scanning. The technology has come a long way. Machines are getting smaller, smarter, and faster. Now you can 3-D model your own piece, your own design. I work with a laptop and the 3-D printer sits on my desk. Using CAD designs and computerized manufacturing instead of manually carving out of wax, I can make parts on my desk.

First I request the actual half of the pair they do have. I take jpeg images for a record and view them on a screen, and then I take the actual piece and have it scanned. If there are complex details, that forces me to use a probe scanner, which has long needles that smoothly pass back and forth over the actual piece, following the radius and the concave areas. This records the points at certain distances on the surface. Ninety-five percent of the time I'll use a setting of every .0002 of an inch, the distance of a hair, ending up with a 3-D point cloud that ranges between 50,000 and 300,000 points. Having captured the point cloud I use 3-D software called Rapidform, which was developed for the 3-D scanning world and also is used in the automotive and space industries. When you are trying to copy something that already exists, you have to be dead on

— and this takes all those points, and connects them as triangles, that join together and form a 3-D mesh of the actual piece. Jewelry is small! I need to keep that tolerance tight.

Then, I upload the scan to a 3-D printer whose small jets spit out, or deposit, small, incredibly slender amounts of wax that create the surface of the model. It reminds me of a spider making its web. Finally, we have the new half of the pair, unless if it has stones that I do by hand. It's impossible to mimic the eye and hand of the jeweler; you can't capture it with a robot even though there is equipment to do stone setting.

Jewelry has to have balance and lightness to be wearable, and a lot of that comes with experience. 3-D modeling is not going to tell you everything. Often a designer renders a design that doesn't work so I streamline a design and guide the designer. If a flower with petals, leaves, and stems is what they want, I'll suggest a hollow back, or if it's quarter-carat diamonds, I will suggest an Omega assembly for the finding, where there is a shepherd's hook type finding but with a clasp around the back. I like to take ideas and bring the jewelry to life so it's comfortable and manufacture-able.

Crowns.
Source: Sarah Feldman.

Pinup, one.
Source: Sarah Feldman.

Sarah Feldman

– Brooklyn, New York

Inexpensive jewelry can be ho-hum, but not Sarah Feldman's imaginative, wearable alternative pairs, which she sells on the Etsy website (froufroubijou) and the sidewalks of New York.

I get my entrepreneurism from my father's side of the family. He started his own software business and was very pleased by my ventures into business at a young age. Sadly, most were failures. I created flower pens, made oven mitt purses, sold candy in high school, and at the end of the day, money was wasted. But even then I learned a lot about the customer's wants and needs. The funny thing was my jewelry business really started as a hobby to decorate no one but myself.

I started my jewelry business in high school. I read magazines like any high school girl and started experimenting, collecting graphics on clothing and jewelry. I loved how new technology at home could create your own line of clothing or jewelry.

I created necklaces, earrings, bracelets for myself using a small hole puncher, printed laminated sheets, and wire. To my surprise, friends and others were interested in my pieces and I started selling at high school for very cheap prices. Senior year I took my items to stores near where I lived, and sold to my first ever store: Lot 8. The store is owned by Project Runway winner Chloe Dao.

Sophomore year of college, I discovered Etsy, and started posting items there. Because of my wonderful clients and customers, my jewelry has evolved and is still evolving. I found my love of public domain imagery and use it in all my pieces. I have over 20,000 public domain pieces of vintage illustrations stored on a hard drive. It is my digital treasure trove. I'm a big fan of Rococo, Art Nouveau, and Art Deco. I also find that my jewelry looks great in the "Steampunk" genre.

Etsy was basically where my hobby became an opportunity. With over six hundred items sold and counting, I have sold all over the world and used any negative feedback to my advantage. I have learned that great communication, shipment, and patience towards each piece is very helpful.

Most of the art in my pieces is of a lost art and technique. Ads you see these days no longer have the glamour of the past. It's as though my jewelry is tiny kitsch art galleries on people's ears. I am not stating that the past was splendid whatsoever — some parts of it were very sad. I do have to say, though: the past had so many beautiful things that were not filled with capitalism. There were more locally-owned stores, family-run businesses. I am hoping my business will have a turning point and I will be able to pay my own rent. If Etsy was around in grandma's time, I bet she would have loved getting her art out while not just being a housewife. It was very hard for her at the time to be considered an artist and female.

Pinup, two.
Source: Sarah Feldman.

Mila Tanya Griebel

– London, England

I am properly stunned by Mila Tanya Griebel's work. This is what real art does — stops us in our quotidian tracks and beckons us to a higher level of experience. Mila lives in London and is represented in museums such as the Jewish Museum in New York, the Jewish Museum in London, and the Victoria & Albert Museum. Much of her work is used for ritual in people's homes and synagogues. Here, Mila shares her perspective on jewelry in our lives.

When I was very young, I would sit and watch my mother, a beauty queen and model, go through the ritual of make-up, hair and earrings framing her face. In the punk era, anything and everything dangled from my lobes.

My work over the last thirty years has developed around Judaica objects used in rituals at home or in the synagogue. I have relied on the study of biblical texts and tried to use the vivid images and narrative they offer in a modern context.

The sun is the source of light, but the moon is the reflected glory — and so much more powerful — because it is seen at night against the darkness of space. As an artist working in precious metals, it is difficult not to pick up on the fundamental meaning of gold and silver representing the sun and moon as they have done throughout the ages in art, poetry, and jewelry. Gold is the most important — the source of wealth echoing the source of light in the sun; but silver is the most important to me as a woman, as it echoes the moon and all that means to the nature of women. This is why I have chosen to use it most in my work as I am much more strongly connected to it than any other metal.

At heart I am a city girl who lived through the urbanization of art, with the punk movement of the Seventies and the graffiti of the Eighties drawing on pop culture roots laid down in the Sixties. Recently there has

Coil.
Source: Mila Griebel.

Runes on silver.
Source: Mila Griebel.

been a revival of a pop art and graffiti fusion, through the likes of Banksy, which is prevalent in London if you look around. I wanted to create a piece of graffiti to wear — a statement that is both oblique and personal as a lot of graffiti art often is. I chose to use the scriptural "to find a virtuous woman is far above rubies" (Proverbs 31:10). It stood out for me on several levels; comparing a woman to a jewel is not unusual, but it is normally obvious jewels, such as diamonds or pearls, whereas rubies have the resonance of blood, life, and death.

Like my work itself, marrying old text with new contexts, these two themes are juxtapositions — light and dark, life and death — with female themes planted at the center of both. This is why I wanted to make earrings, as they, too, are dual and culturally attached to women's self-expression.

Source: Stephanie Kilgast.

Source: Stephanie Kilgast.

Source: Stephanie Kilgast.

Stephanie Kilgast

– Vannes, France

Earrings that are micro-versions of objects, like charms on a bracelet, are common, but Stephanie Kilgast, as a miniaturist sculptor, is in a class of her own.

Working, and in a sense living, in a Lilliputian world feels like playing giant all the time. The women who will wear my earrings are playful and a tad childish. Not in the sense of being stupid or doing stupid things, but just as enthusiastic about the beauty of their lives and keen on colorful and fun accessories.

The more I sculpt in miniature, the more I realize what I absolutely love about it is working with colors and textures. I've always been drawn to abstract painting like Kandinsky's (to name just one artist) and am very attracted to colorful street art. My whole life revolves around colors so that really is something I pursue in my work and photography.

I also love putting lots of details on a small surface; I can't help it. As much as I like clean geometric designs, I'm just unable to do them because I always want to add more details to my work (which is, of course, fitting for miniature replicas of food).

Another thing that really grew with time is the sense of joy my work gives to people. They feel like children again, want to play, find my work cute or adorable, and it just makes them smile. And that appreciation, that happiness is something that gives meaning to my work.

Because as an artist, especially an artist living in France, I always feel I have to improve, make it better, put some meaning in my work, make it more powerful. But at the end of the day, I just enjoy to sculpt in miniature and with lots of colors, because it makes me happy, and I've come to accept that "being happy" is truly the only goal in life one can have.

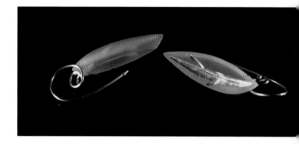

Leaves.
Source: Karen McCreary.

Karen McCreary

– Long Beach, California

Karen McCreary's earrings are inventive, fun, and color-ful — as well as meticulously crafted. She sells in galleries and at shows.

As an art major in college, I took a jewelry class on a whim and it was the start of a life-long passion. That training also led to a job in jewelry manufacturing, giving me not just a new medium for artistic expression, but a career path. The cost of traditional materials motivated me to experiment, and the color, transparency, and workability of plastics have made it my medium of choice for years. It also allows me to make piec-es that are more affordable and the value of which is derived more from my creativity than the value of the materials.

I am inspired by the scientific impulse to observe, ex-plore, and describe. I also love the small scale of jewelry and using the human body as my canvas. It's always a thrill to see people wearing my work out in the world, like a moving public art installation.

My jewelry combines plastics, metals, and color. I am drawn to these materials because of their transparency, depth, and movement of light and color through the surfaces. My pieces are primarily acrylic, which is hand-carved and fabricated. The carved areas are internally lit or layered with a colored lacquer, giving a feeling of mystery to the light reflected throughout the clear forms. I then create metal elements to complement and complete the pieces. The Bubble Dangle is carved acrylic with 22-carat gold leaf and gold-filled ear wires. The Leaf Dangle is carved acrylic with 22-carat gold leaf and sterling silver.

Jewelry is an art form loaded with meanings. In my work, I explore light, mood, and illusion while combining contemporary and traditional materials and techniques. It is an investment, a token of love, a symbol of power or wealth. Like electronic devices that enhance the senses and capabilities, jewelry is an instrument that, while wearing it, can make you feel more beau-tiful, powerful, and desirable than without it. These associations fascinate me and attract me to creating jewelry as a means of personal expression.

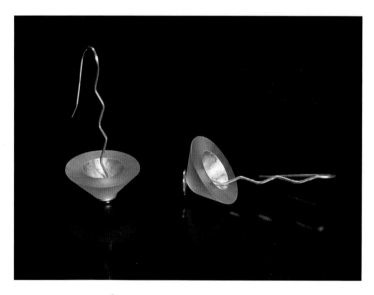

Green cones.
Source: Karen McCreary.

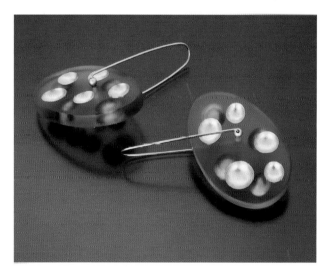

Bubbles.
Source: Karen McCreary.

Source: Laurence
Nelson.

Source: Laurence
Nelson.

Source: Laurence
Nelson.

Laurence Nelson

– west of Boston, Massachusetts

Laurence Nelson, owner of Global Odyssey Design, is primarily a silversmith who gathers his materials around the globe. I tracked him for months, receiving many messages like this to my final subject line of the email, "Where art thou?"... Hi Jane, I am on a small road called Monkey Forest Road, which actually ends in a monkey forest. Bali is amazing. I love the magic, spirit, reverence. I will be home by the end of February.

I have been creating jewelry for more than thirty years, since I discovered, and fell in love with, sterling silver. I was working as a photojournalist, having taught myself photography in college. This carried me across North America, then Europe, and eventually to the Middle East. In Jerusalem, I began making simple silver pieces and selling them outside one of the spectacular gates to the old city.

Since then I have continued to learn other aspects of silversmithing, from forging to casting. My early training as a photographer has been an invaluable aid in composition, balance, color, and attention to detail. Carefully chosen gemstones and cultured pearls have become signature elements in my work, and I am continually seeking new materials to work with, such as shards of antique Chinese porcelain, cut woods, coral, and old coins from around the world.

My designs are predominantly classical. I find ideas and inspiration in books of jewelry design going back 7,000 years.

Hummingbirds.
Source: Judith Rudolph.

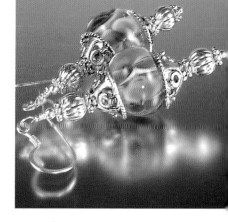

Flowers.
Source: Judith Rudolph.

Judith Rudolph

– Thomaston, Maine

In a Hasidic tale, a poor rabbi in Krakow dreams he is to seek a treasure in the capital, Prague, under a bridge that leads to the king's palace. When he gets there, he is denied passage across the bridge, but a friendly captain of the guards hears the rabbi's story and says that he too had a strange dream of a treasure under the stove of a poor Jew in Krakow. The rabbi returns to his own home to find the great treasure. I looked through hundreds of online stores (in itself enjoyable) and was captivated by Holly Cottage Designs, an Internet store of a retired editor who makes swimmingly beautiful earrings, in a neighboring town to where I live on the Maine coast. Here is what she told me in answers to questions about her joyous earrings.

My tagline used to be "Artisan Jewelry that Celebrates Feminine Style"; my work often has a feminine — okay, girlie — look but I hope a more sophisticated one. I'm inspired by my love of gardening, sunshine, ice crystals on my window, and observations of the little things. I'm crazy about glitter and I love to play with color combinations. I'm sensitive to color and rely on my visceral feelings around it when creating jewelry.

I'm entirely self-taught. When I wanted to learn a certain technique, I read about it and then practiced, practiced, practiced. I get to work at home and my work table is in a wonderful, big, sunny room with a sensational view. My office lies adjacent, so I get to hear my Google Notifier ding when a customer buys something, or has a question. It is also perfectly quiet, something that's essential to my wellbeing. Our cats often sleep on the windowsills in my workroom, recharging their batteries in the sun for their next attack on my loose beads. Just looking at them makes me feel happy.

Each week I spend hours searching the Internet for lampwork beads to use in my jewelry. There are hundreds of work-at-home lampwork artists who sell their original beads online. Over the years I've learned what to look for in quality and design. Of course, that intuitive thing comes first. I just know when a bead's colors and design are right for me. My table is covered with boxes of components. I start by pulling out some element that happens to appeal to me at that moment — a bead, a gemstone, and so forth — and then I play! I might make six or seven versions of an earring, necklace, or bracelet, then dismantle it before the "aha" combination appears, and I know the piece is done. Balance has a lot to do with what makes it right, but that's usually an entirely subconscious factor. One of the challenges that I had to learn the hard way was keeping true to myself with my designs. In the beginning I thought it would be a good idea to try to follow the latest fads. I spent too much time looking at other people's work and found I was being influenced to veer off my own path. Not only did these pieces not sell very well, but they were sapping the joy out of my work.

I make a variety of lengths and styles of dangle earrings. Some customers love the long, flashy ones while others prefer shorter, more classic styles. And I'm glad because if there's anything that spoils the creative process, it's repetition.

It amazes me to have customers from all over the world. A typical example happened a few weeks ago when a regular customer in Germany asked if I could duplicate for her a pair of earrings that was listed in my online shop as sold. I love to spoil my customers and I was delighted to fulfill her request, but I don't keep a large inventory of components because I rarely duplicate a piece. The earrings she wanted were composed of glass beads from a lampwork artist in Australia, gold-plated ear posts shaped like branches from South Korea, more gold findings from Bali, and crystals made in Austria (and, of course, they were designed and created in Maine, USA). It took a couple of weeks to receive everything I needed for this one pair of earrings; but, really, what fun to think of all the hands involved.

Joan Son

– Houston, Texas

Joan Son is an origami master and paper sculptor, who makes festive earrings especially around Christmas. They look as though they could go from tree decorations to the ears. The line between sculpture and fashion is simply erased by her earrings.

I am passionate about paper. I get excited when my grocery list includes paper towels or napkins. What new patterns will I find? Just getting close to the paper aisle raises my pulse! I work in paper with a discipline in origami. I use the finest papers in the world and some of the poorest quality as well. Each one has a feel that sets the mood or alters the image of whatever I am working on.

For years I resisted making earrings. Oh, everyone makes earrings, I said. Plenty of that. Surely my art is more important. One year a friend convinced me to try. Okay, I said, and I found that the papers made small sculptural pieces — discs, squares, and rectangles — perfect for decorating the ears. And lightweight. I could create large elaborate earrings and they would feel like nothing. It was fun. And people bought them. And they asked for more until it seemed if all I did was make earrings I could live well.

My ideas have continued to evolve over the years. First with Japanese papers and origami models, and then simple geometric shapes and photos of the Buddha's eyes. Even solid background colors from the pages of Tiffany & Co. catalogs were in my palette. This year I began using the pages from Japanese storybooks. I love the shape of the characters and wonder about the stories they tell. No paper is off limits to me. I see the ideas everywhere. The glass and metal beads are only there to set off the wonderful papers.

Here are some steps I take to make earrings:

Paper is generally thin so I glue two sheets together. Sometimes a third sandwich of paper in between is required to hold a good solid shape. I glue these together in pieces about five inches square. Not too large. Small enough to press in heavy books and dry overnight. For glue I use a good quality acid-free gel medium. I brush it on one side of the paper and quickly set it on the second. Press out all the extra glue with a bone folder until it is smooth. I use sheets of wax paper on either side so the glue will not get on the book pages. Plus it is easy to peel these sheets from the wax paper if any glue sneaks out.

After these pieces are dry and solid, I brush them with an acrylic medium from the hardware store. It is non-yellowing and very protective of the papers. I coat one side at a time, being sure that one dries before I turn it over to coat the second.

When all that is dry, I begin cutting shapes... circles, squares, rectangles. I use my Exacto blade on a hard rubber matt with straight edge. For circles I use a fine quality Japanese circle cutter. After cutting I carefully coat the edges of these shapes with more acrylic medium so no raw paper is exposed.

I design the earrings. This is the most fun part. I gather all these odd shapes and sizes on my work table with the glass and metal beads to accent. I begin to put the pieces together until the design works. Generally I make each earring a little different so the set is asymmetrical.

Now, the task of using the appropriate findings to hold the earrings together and attach the ear wires begins. Where links are required to go through the paper beads I use a fine Japanese hole punch...really a book-binding tool. Making a tiny hole on one or two sides of the paper bead is determined by the design.

Buddha.
Source: Joan Son.

Sampler.
Source: Joan Son.

Cranes.
Source: Joan Son.

Squares and
circle.
Source: Joan Son.

What's next?

Maybe I will graduate to plastic. I'll use those funny orange pieces that come on the ink cartridges for my printer or the theatrical gels that cover hot lights. Found objects I think. When my husband and I are on a walk in the neighborhood and I look down, he says, "Don't pick that up." I usually do.

Erik Stewart

– Tucson, Arizona

If you want to prove a man indifferent to earrings, generally that they are wearable sculpture, show him the work of Erik Stewart. I see them, architectural yet feminine, on Marlene Dietrich or Charlize Theron. Erik is early in his career, but it seems it must have taken him a century to develop his art, which he speaks about here.

I view myself as a jewelry designer. I can create jewelry and sell it; however, my passion is designing. I specialize in 18-carat gold, palladium, and platinum. I also work with sterling silver and stainless steel. I personally prefer working with the high-end precious metals, as their richness, rarity, sustainability, and color are of great value. Gold, palladium, and platinum are supreme for strength, durability, and malleability as well as their being non-oxidizing elements.

My mother is a former jewelry instructor, now an independent jewelry designer, and my father is an architect. I believe my work reflects my parents' attributes. I find myself learning when it comes to manufacturing jewelry, but even more with running a business. Creating a successful business and brand has been my biggest challenge as I am by nature an artist.

Ideas and inspirations visit me in various ways; from music, nature, and architecture to a first glance at an object before a second glance occurs.

Earrings should be lightweight, and non-allergenic materials are required. Regardless of the elements or materials used, these are my two filters before composing a pair of earrings.

My technique for creating jewelry typically begins with a rough sketch derived from an idea or vague visual that will later be refined from a concept into a practical wearable object (what I call Art for the Body). This stage will determine colors, materials, engineering hurdles, and whether customization is possible. From there I draft the design on the computer to create a

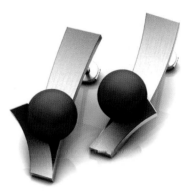

Purple on silver folds.
Source: Erik Stewart.

precise model. This digital model may now go through a 3-D printing process, unless there's feasibility to fabricate, then I'll take that route.

Everything is made by me or with the help of my skilled master jewelers. My work is unique and each piece is specific in many ways.

Fluted baskets.
Source: Erik Stewart.

Coral flowers.
Source: Valentina
St. Gielar.

St. Gielar
sapphire drops.
Source: Valentina
St. Gielar.

White flowers.
Source: Valentina St. Gielar.

Ian and Valentina St. Gielar

– Hollywood, Florida

The examples of Ian St. Gielar's glass and bead jewelry are nonpareil, and, since Ian passed, Valentina continues Stanley Hagler NYC & Co., which is the St. Gielar line. St. Gielar jewelry conjures up gorgeous extravagance without being expensive considering the classic style and workmanship.

Born in Sanok, Poland in 1953, Ian traveled around Europe for years before coming to the United States. His first job was at the Diplomat Resort, and the Hollywood, Florida, area was the only home he knew in America. Ian met Stanley Hagler, became friends with him, and sometime later was invited to work in the Hagler studio here in South Florida, where Hagler had moved from New York City.

The costume jewelry Ian was doing used techniques that were very much like the Miriam Haskell style in terms of coloring and multi-layers, which is no wonder as Hagler started his studio in an attempt to be "better than Haskell." When Ian quickly began to develop an independent style, one of Hagler's valued buyers reacted to seeing his work the first time by signing a new contract for a quarter-million dollars, but with the condition that the jewelry would be designed by Ian.

I came to the United States in 1998 and almost right away was introduced to Ian in his home studio (Hagler passed away in 1996) by mutual friends. In Russia, I had worked as an oil painting artist in a factory of a traditional Russian folk craft of painting on metal. Hearing my background, Ian asked me to work with him — to combine our knowledge and experience to discover new possible styles. I agreed. Nothing came of that! What really happened was that Ian taught me, with great passion. Not only was it a fun process for both of us, laughing for hours and entertaining others with our mixture of English, Russian, and (his) Polish, but we became friends and spent time outside the studio together. What

St. Gielar white and gold pearls.
Source: The Corning Museum of Glass.

Chevron necklace
and earrings.
Source: Valentina St. Gielar.

I brought to Ian's design style was smaller pieces with different details. We also started to use not-so-traditional materials and pieces. My asymmetrical designs would sometimes put him into a state of near shock!

Our technique on a very base level resembles Miriam Haskell's. Seed beads are put on a thin gold- or gold-tone plated brass wire, which is then wrapped around brass (gold-plated for most parts) findings. These wrapped parts are assembled and layered up on a gold-plated brass filigree used as a base, all tied with different thicknesses of plated brass wire and secured with some headpins. The headpins are either Swarovski with crystal heads or old Japanese headpins (a stock bought decades ago) with glass heads of various sizes and colors. Sometimes regular brass head and eye pins are used as well. Then all the parts and pieces are layered up and put together with ties of the headpins on the other side of the base filigree. To finish a medallion so it's wearable, another filigree part, most often of the same type as the base, goes onto the back, covering all the ties and holding some kind of locking or closure. Nametags usually go on the packing filigree too.

All our pieces are unique and there are no two identical. Alike maybe, made after the same general model, the reference design. And many are true one-of-a-kind pieces impossible to repeat. When two jewelers work together, there will be conflict. Period. Ian was a highly talented designer yet always encouraged me to create on my own. Where we often disagreed was scale. His concern was couture as he carried out his vision of exquisite art. Being a woman, I make jewelry that is more on the comfortable, wearable side, although I hope the pieces are still costume jewelry art.

Yahhazie

– Blackfoot, Idaho

Yahhazie (who uses the business name Shoshoneways) makes earrings and moccasins with quills and Czech glass beads. Anyone who has pulled porcupine quills from a dog's coat knows they are slippery and unmanageable. Yahhazie's creations represent perfect quillwork and abound in personality.

My name is Cindi Menta Isaac, I am Shoshone. In 1983, I adopted the name Yahhazie, which means "Little Rock-Chuck" as my dad's nickname is Rock-Chuck. I have plucked more porcupines than I'd like to mention. Porcupines are docile and slow-moving. Quills are hairs that have thickened and are used by porcupines to protect themselves. There are many different lengths and thicknesses of quills in an average porcupine. I have been poked many times by porcupine quills. Years ago I even sat on one and had to have it surgically removed. When you have that happen, it only happens once!

I started beading professionally in 1982, and started making porcupine quill earrings and many other Native American beaded crafts at my kitchen table. My beadwork moments are prayerful. I would be what they call a Prayer Warrior. The many hours that I do beads allow me to spend much of my time communing with Creator. I am honored to be able to share my Native traditions and humbled by the gift of hands.

Shoshone beadwork is some of the finest beadwork the world has to offer, both geometricals and florals. With thirty years of moccasin making and regalia making, the designs are etched in my mind already. I don't really do patterns; I see them in my mind, and base many upon our Shoshone geometrical designs. I don't think anyone really ever masters beadwork; it's the other way around...your beadwork masters you. You want every piece you produce to glorify Creator, and celebrate your ancestors before you. Our ancestors are our teachers, and we are what they left behind. My teacher

Quill-worked.
Source: Yahhazie.

Quill-worked.
Source: Yahhazie.

was Cecila Osbourne LaVatta, my grandmother. She, in her own right, had a wonderful, long life. When she was alive, she was the oldest living relative of Sacajawea. The time that I spent learning beading from her are the moments that make her alive in me. In this we honor our ancestors. Every piece...in my mind I say...May this honor you, Granny!

Each earring has tails and the turquoise ones illustrated here (on previous page) have eleven tails. Tails 2 to 10 have graduated white-tip quills in them. They are different lengths. I used these in the earrings so people could see that not all quills are black-tipped, and that white-tipped quills are equally beautiful. The coral and red squares of the other pair are average length quills. On the black and red ones, I used mostly cut (faceted) seed beads. I chose Native colors as I do love to bead boldly.

Quill-worked.
Source: Yahhazie.

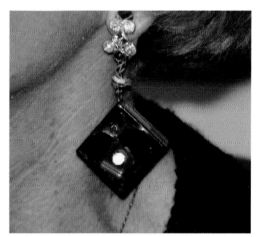

Arousal-detecting sensor.
Source: Ken Aricola, Richard Morton, and John Ross.

Ken Aricola, Richard Morton, and John Ross
– California

Ken Aricola, Richard Morton, and John Ross took out a patent 6277079 for earrings that flash in sync with the wearer's heartbeat. The day after the patent was assigned, the New York Times *mentioned the invention: "Earrings that flash in sync with the wearer's heartbeat — you'll be able to tell if she's glad to see you."*

When the heart beats with a variation, the earring lights up. The lover is able to detect the growing excitement of the partner. The patent also indicated a medical monitor. The prototype for medical-monitoring jewelry came from goldsmith, teacher, and designer, Mary Ann Scherr, who made titanium for colored jewelry in the early 1980s. The metal forms a film related to the body's electric charges and distinct color forms. Commissioned to make a spacesuit costume for Miss Wisconsin to celebrate the first moon landing, Scherr made a stainless-steel belt that simulated the devices that would measure the astronaut's vital signs. The next day she came up with the idea of measuring the body in a similar way on earth and began to make body monitors that were jewelry.

The first body monitor was a cosmetic cover-up for the medical alert equipment for problems of the throat and esophagus. The second monitor Scherr developed was a bracelet that indicated the pre-set pulse rate of the wearer: a light emitting diode [LED] displayed the ongoing pulse beat, and a marked change in heart rhythms triggered a beep, which alerted the wearer to call the medics. Scherr's line of "medical jewelry" now includes a pendant music box alarm that plays "Smoke Gets in Your Eyes," warning people with respiratory problems of even minute traces of smoke, and a breath monitor concealed in a silver choker whose six lights flash on when the wearer has consumed too much alcohol.

Romances are for a certain mood when you are mulling over love. A typical interlude might be... The girl in red waltzing in his arms had the Duke's complete attention. A fragrance like jasmine came from her long luxuriant hair, enticing him. The slight shift of her cheeks and turn of her slender neck enchained him as they danced. As the Duke gazed at the ingénue's countenance, the tiny flower of garnets in her ears seemed to flash at him with every heartbeat, attesting to the effect of the contact of their bodies. If I were sure, he thought, I would make love to her now before I depart on the morrow for the Azores.

What if the Duke could really detect the course of her arousal? According to one of the inventors, John Ross, a patent attorney, the patent is still available, as the prototype ("the size of two pennies tacked together") was licensed to an R&D firm that made a few thousand, but decided production costs were too high to make it under twenty dollars for teenagers.

The technique for monitoring blood with an infrared light source is well known. At the doctor's office, the person sticks a finger in the slot and the device illuminates the finger with infrared light, which passes through the skin and measures the flow of blood by the infrared rays bouncing back to the sensor. The earring has a pulsed photocell, a sensor, and a light. When the photocell and sensor detect a heartbeat, they activate the light so it flashes. One design has the transmitter and sensor on the side of the lobe and the other on either side. The signals are collected, continually, making the sensor go up and down as the blood flows. A threshold is built into the electronic circuits so when the signal increases the LED light goes on and the earring blinks.

Women Talk About their Earrings

> "What we reach for and what ultimately touches us is the radiance we've projected on things, not the things themselves."

~ Andre Aciman, *Alibis*

to buy a triple strand of Jackie Kennedy-style pearls, with a diamond clasp...and of course I had to have the pearl and diamond earrings to go with them. It was that very pair of earrings that started my lifetime collection of them. But the pain of those clips!

Back in my hometown of Hollywood, I graduated as a young actress to gold loops and found a pair that went on in a little twisty way, which made it look like your ears were pierced. I was starting to like that look, but was stuck with that, "Oh no, not my ears, no holes for me!" I remember arriving on the set to do a guest lead on *Star Trek* and being fitted for my little red yeoman uniform wearing those very earrings, and when we commenced to film, they were nixed. Maybe the thinking was all those hundreds of years into the future, would women still be wearing them? Later, when they used my character for the "Star Trek Barbie," Barbie ended up wearing my little gold loops, even though I couldn't.

It took my daughter, Cami, to convince me to get my ears pierced and we did it together. We went to the home of a dear friend whose husband was, and still is, an ear, nose, and throat specialist, and he brought his little piercing gadget home with him, and pierced our ears for us in their den.

We graduated to wearing diamond or pearl studs for a while and then I discovered "big." The '80s were here and to go with all those shoulder pads that Norma Kamali inflicted on us, we needed big hair and earrings to go with it.

At the time I was married to a man who was well-off and I collected some lovely earrings from a Beverly Hills jeweler, such as studs of emeralds, rubies, and diamonds. I designed a circle of pavé diamonds to encircle the studs, and they were interchangeable: if you wanted more diamonds, you wore the little circles around the studs. After we divorced, a light went off in my head. "Bling!" I thought. "With the creation of cubic zirconia who needs real?"

I could get five-carat cubic zirconia studs with pear-shaped drops dangling from them, which rivaled Oprah's. Who knew? Did my friends carry a loupe around with them?

As time passed, the copies of fine jewels got even better; they were becoming state-of-the-art, and I learned you could find gorgeous earrings for $19.95. Some were so fun they didn't need to look real. And that is how I amassed a collection of every color and style. I have kitty earrings that look like my Tonkinese cats, which have beautiful aqua eyes, and so forth. I discovered how divine it is to shop in stores where East Indians display and sell their jewelry and they are exact replicas of the earrings a Maharani would wear, as they use those same divine molds to make the copies.

What do I wear every day? Thin but big gold wire loops are my signature earrings, but, on occasion, a pair of the hundreds in little boxes on my shelves comes out, and with a little polish or dip in hot soapy water, I put those posts through my ear holes that were run through at the doctor's home so many years ago.

ELISE BLACK
A sculptor known for outdoor installations and a painter, Elise is a stunning natural redhead.

I love earrings and gravitate to dangling pairs so that they don't get lost in my long curls. While I understand the concept of "less is more," when it comes to adorning oneself with jewelry, I am an artist and often like more.

I don't feel like I am fully dressed unless I have a set of dangling baubles in my ear. I think that earrings enhance a woman's beauty because they can reflect light to the eyes and hair. I also believe that since people look (hopefully!) at your face when they talk to you, they are reading something about your personal style by your choice of jewelry.

SHERRY GOODMAN LUTTRELL
A stylish art historian and lecturer in San Francisco, Sherry has never pierced her ears. She was born in Providence, Rhode Island, where her father owned a jewelry manufacturing company whose catalogs we paged through in college.

Earrings always involve loss: losing an earring is something that anyone who loves, likes, or simply wears earrings knows comes with the territory. But for those like myself who have refrained from piercing their ears, it is a predictable liability, if almost always a rueful surprise.

A pierced earring is lost if mislaid — a clip-on or screw-back earring is lost, typically irretrievably, by slipping off one's earlobe. Mislaid can be at home, thus potentially found. Slipping off almost invariably occurs when the wearer is out and about, often oblivious to the loss, thus lost for good.

However self-evidently practical the practice of ear-piercing now appears, fashion has fluctuated with regards to this age-old, globe-spanning custom. When I was a child growing up in a Rhode Island neighborhood largely populated by second-generation Italian immigrants, Italian-American girls had pierced ears, which by socio-economic association were considered déclassé.

By my twenties and thirties, fashion had shifted. The way tattoos are now ubiquitous, no longer associated with sailors, pierced ears had increasingly become the norm. But by then a certain stubbornness had set in. The more earrings I lost, the more I felt invested in maintaining my un-pierced condition. Gripped by a kind of contrary, good-money-after-bad determination that, having already lost numerous beloved earrings, I would hold fast to my position and not capitulate. Moreover, the older I got, the larger my clip-on earring wardrobe, almost none of it amenable to being changed over to pierced. Admittedly, I never did take much to the idea of first piercing and then keeping open a hole, regardless of how small, in my ear (so small, of course, in comparison with today's infinitely more extreme, if much less common, practice of inserting graduated plugs that eventually turn the earlobe into a droopy loop when not filled).

My childhood experience of earrings was marked by the pleasure of playing with my mother's, a sort of manual daydreaming through the contents of her jewelry box. Her earrings — dating to the '40s and '50s — were typically screw-backs, in theory adjustable, but somehow always too loose (cf. losing the earring) or too tight (ouch).

Today I own a few pairs (inherited from my mother) and can almost never hit the acceptable, comfortable, middle ground; I suspect it doesn't exist.

Now I look back and wonder how did women wear genuinely valuable gems back then? Surely not by insecurely screwing or clipping them on. My mother's collection of elegant earrings must perforce have all been costume jewelry, not real jewels — except for a garnet, and another opal, pair — and thus acceptably lose-able. While I recall if not her earrings, her rings were "real."

Actually I spent so much time pawing through my mother's jewelry, especially pieces kept in a large velvet heart-shaped box, that I recall her earrings as well as I do those from my own past. In particular, one oddly popular motif (she had three such pairs!): a small basket with a faux pearl "egg," suspended by tiny chains from a screw-back (I still have a pair that I never wear). She also owned some clip-ons: one pair, a cluster of faux amethysts; another of classic rhinestone "diamonds" — both, now in my much less elegant jewelry box and occasionally clipped on to my own ears. Perhaps playing with my mother's earrings is the source of my predilection for clip-on/screw-back.

Actually before leaving my mother's jewelry box, let me run to mine and see what of hers I have there:

- A screw-back pair of double fire-orange opals
- Two variations of the aforementioned faux amethyst clip-ons (with several of the stones fallen out and replaced). I don these every so often and then their weightiness makes me change my mind.
- A fragile pair of screw-back chartreuse enamel flower-petaled earrings — little floral touches that look like Hawaii but probably date to her time in Cuba

Even when one does not actually lose a clip-on and retrieves it immediately after it slips off, one is fated for earring repair. I own one (initially) inexpensive pair of platinum-colored clip-on disks whose back has detached from the disk more times than I can count, i.e., almost every time one falls and hits the ground. Eventually glue no longer held: my local jewelry repairer resorted to soldering (which wrinkled the faux silver finish) at $20 per earring. At the end of all this gluing and soldering, I'd invested $100 in these $20 earrings! However, some dropped clip-ons are irreparable — I think of a midnight-blue faceted glass clip-on that shattered the first time it fell and the faux-ivory drop earring that broke into small pieces.

At this point I could (but won't) indulge in a litany of individual lost earrings, as I surely remember each and every one. The one pair that comes immediately to mind — perhaps the first of the losses — was a true treasure: good-sized, bronze-toned pendant earrings I found and fell in love with decades ago in a small shop in Portugal. I can still picture their exceptional subtlety — the intricate twisted metalwork hung with small metallic spheres in a slightly darker shade of bronze. I lost one within only a month or two. So beautiful was the remaining one that I was tempted to, but didn't, wear it alone.

In the world of earrings, nothing is sadder to behold than the widowed one, no longer wearable but a full-fledged reminder of the loss. A single earring is all too emblematic of the clip-on/screw-back genre.

Meanwhile, it has become almost impossible to find new earrings that are *not* for pierced ears. At the earring shop Jest Jewels, I ask for any clip-ons — none! Thank heavens for the higher-end jewelry designer Alexis Bittar, who fashions some of his hallmark, softly-glowing Lucite numbers as clip-ons (and with the added luxury of little rubber covers to soften the pressure on the earlobe).

I continue to trek doggedly back and forth to the jewelry repair shop, sometimes with new pierced earrings that need to be changed to clip-ons, and sometimes with the latest clip-on to crash to earth and separate from its clip. I'm still immune to the lure of pierced ears, happy with my diminishing (and never the "real thing") wardrobe of clip-on earrings.

ANTOINETTE MAITLINS
International gem and jewelry expert and author Antoinette Matlins gives a surprising answer to "What is your favorite pair?"

My favorite pair of earrings are simple large round natural pearl studs, not cultured. Natural pearls are the most precious gems throughout history, and these are old white lustrous saltwater pearls from the Persian Gulf. My engagement ring is a natural pearl too, mid-1800s, with the pearl at the center. I see pearls as a very significant metaphor for life because they are the result of having to overcome a life-threatening challenge, through which something of beauty, and precious on every level, is created. When the mollusk processes it, it overcomes a challenge to its existence. The organism can give up or die — or create something never created, without a challenge, of great beauty and charm. Life is not about what's easy, but how we take what we are dealt and turn it into beauty, or become overpowered and give an ugly response. When I look at my engagement ring, I'm reminded it's the actions we take that create a pearl. I have one on either side of my face, on my head, and the symbolism is in my thoughts. The reminder is poignant and strong.

The pearl is also the first gem associated with love. Krishna descended and gave a pearl to his daughter on her wedding day. It was a Renaissance wedding gift, and Venus was born from the pearl-producing scallop, as depicted by Botticelli. The connection to love and life for me betokens our active determination to have lives of beauty and radiance.

SUSI HAUSER
Susi is a wise woman. A retired dean at an Ivy League college, she exemplifies, in my view, unerring and elegant taste. When Susi was a small child, Hitler annexed Austria, and her distinguished family escaped to America. This is the backdrop to what she says about piercing.

Ornamentation of the body occurs in every era and in every culture. Earlobes provide the most readily available body part and the most convenient. Earrings signal economic level, age, and taste. Most of all they signal group identity — for instance, Black power, WASP restraint, Jewish new wealth. Earrings, of course, have their iconography and iconology. One sees Christmas trees, pumpkins, skeletons, et al.

Young girls wear small gold spheres. *Grandes dames* wear large pearls. The hierarchy of cost is clear: silver to gold, garnets to rubies, aquamarine to emerald.

Today in our culture not wearing earrings means just as much as wearing them and makes a similarly significant statement.

As a young person, I felt that piercing one's ears was primitive and barbaric. When I was about 21, however, I decided I wanted pierced ears. My father, a physician, obtained special, gold earrings, which could be used to pierce the ears and be left in the ear as earrings. He pierced my ears. The holes were very asymmetrical. He had to do it again.

Since then, I have worn earrings everyday. I have conservative, simple earrings. I have artsy-craftsy silver earrings. I have Mexican and Native American earrings. I choose my earrings to match and complement my outfit. My favorite earrings are half-domes made of brushed white gold. I wear them everyday with my swimsuit for my water exercise class.

LAURA

Laura just smiles when someone compliments her on her earrings.

They are flash-drives and have different information related to my studies and personal life. I bought them at Staples with the eyes already, and added the hooks. They do not, as someone suggested, correspond to right and left brain.

They were pretty easy to assemble: I bought two mini-USB drives from Staples. I then took four jump rings (two sets of two) and looped both through the little hoop on the end of the USB drive, using needle-nose pliers. It's important to attach two jump hoops, because one will inevitably slip. (With two jump rings, all you have to do is re-attach

one; with one, you have to run around looking for your lost USB drive.) The third and last step is simply to attach one fishhook earring to each set of jump hoops.

I created the earrings out of necessity: while working for four different employers at five locations, I spend very little time at home and end up doing a lot of work at the computer lab during breaks and between jobs. At first, I carried a normal flashdrive in my pocket. After the third close call with my washing machine, I decided that was no longer an option and created the earrings.

I haven't yet adorned the earrings in any way, although I have thought of painting them to look like the "Lego" people they so closely resemble in shape. I have added a tiny red dot to one of them, to indicate which one contains the files that are an exact copy of my home computer files, as opposed to the right-ear earring, which is just used for temporary files while working in the lab.

CHERYL IRELAND HOOPER

Cheryl lives in San Francisco and has a store, Cheryl Antiques, also called Vignette on Ruby Lane. When she told me about "borrowing" antique poissardes from her own stock, I asked her about them, and include her reply, which shows the flair of many antiquarian jewelers for description.

My personal love affair with earrings began when I was about three years old. My Portuguese immigrant grandmother always wore them, not fancy ones, just simple gold hoops. To my eye they were beautiful and exotic. I pleaded with my mother to let me have my ears pierced so I could replicate the look, but she said no. It was the early 1950s, and there was a different "ear aesthetic" if you will — think clip-ons and screw-backs.

I waited impatiently until I was a rebellious fifteen-year-old and then I asked my best friend to pierce my ears one night while babysitting, after the kids were in bed. Heck, she had done her own the month before, by herself in front of the bathroom mirror. I wasn't that brave, but, with her help, mission accomplished. Anticipating my mother's displeasure, I tried, unsuccessfully, to hide my ears under my hair. But it was too late and I was never going back.

Earrings are still my favorite jewelry article, and if I could only have one pair, they would be gold hoops. I have had a jewelry shop for twenty-five years and very rarely have I worn a pair from my stock. I did "borrow" from stock *poissarde* earrings to wear to a friend's book launch recently. They are of the long, semi-circular wire *poissarde*-style (as opposed to having an S-shaped finding). They have thin rose gold sheets, beautifully cut and curled at the top edges, hand-chased and set with a single white pearl each. Etched foliate shapes in green gold accent the top portions and two-prong set old-cut diamonds each are set north and south. Decorative horizontal bars, attached just below the halfway point behind the rose gold plaques, add attractive detailing and dimension. These are hallmarked with French marks from the city of Perrone and made just before 1800. Wearing a pair of old earrings gives you a different, new orientation, and I saw these were easy to get on and so comfortable — not heavy. They felt wonderful on all night.

At the Heart of Collecting...

One day my daughter Julia emailed me. She had stopped by my house and wondered if it was okay to borrow my ruby red earrings for her date — or were they too valuable?

The faceted studs tipped with a dot of gold were dime-store, but I loved the idea of her sending me this photo as a question. It made me feel close to her as I was to my own mother when I peered into her jewelry box.

Gay Talese ... A Man's Perspective

As well as a legendary journalist, my friend Gay Talese has a prominent, attractive wife and two sophisticated daughters, and is often on "best dressed" lists. When I asked him about earrings, I should have known he would begin with someone of great importance in our society.

When I think of earrings, I think of handsome black men, none more handsome and talented than Michael Jordan. He offset his gold ring that punctured his left ear by shaving his head, and so all you had was the combined shine of his glistening face (sweating through a fourth-quarter comeback) and that glistening circular ring, the gold itself bearing his spectacular sweat.

About earrings for women I never much thought about it and certainly never bought earrings for women, most particularly for my wife, who regularly loses the ones she buys for herself, if indeed she did buy them for herself. Who knows if lovers of other men's wives are more generous than a woman's longtime spouse? Anyway, I believed long ago that spending money on jewelry was risky and unwise, especially if the jewelry was small and easily lost — lost perhaps in a hotel bed during an afternoon tryst.

Earrings 101

text by **Leslie S. George** and **Cindy L. Konney**

New England Gemological Laboratory

drawings by **David L. Arnheim**

A preference for certain gems has nothing to do with expertise — it has to do with aesthetic appeal — which is subjective and simply a matter of personal taste. Like anything in nature or art, beauty is in the eyes of the beholder.

Round cut gems are now, and have been throughout time, the most common shape and easiest to set, as are the other more common shapes found in earrings — drops and briolettes — that hang and are uniquely well-suited for earrings .

Besides diamonds and pearls, rubies, sapphires, and emeralds — referred to as "The Big Three" — are the most commonly found gemstones in earrings, especially in the United States. There have been periods of time, like during the Victorian Era, when gems like garnet and amethyst were favored. The popularity of a particular gemstone has to do with taste, fashion, and its availability in the marketplace. Many gemstones gain popularity when they are first discovered (like demantoid garnet or tanzanite) or when new mine sources are found.

Careful restoration of antique earrings should not decrease their value.

DETERMINING AN EARRING'S AGE

Earring backings can sometimes serve as a clue that can help you determine the age of an earring. The key word here is "clue." "Shepherd crook" (commonly called "fish hook") wires have been used since ancient times — and are still in use today. Hinged kidney wire, threaded posts, and screw backs began to be used in the late nineteenth century, so, if you find earrings with these backings, you know they can't be older than that. However, it isn't a definitive way to date the earrings, because although they may have been made in 1900 — they may also have been made in 2000!

There was actually a period of time when earrings were made out of hummingbirds and feathers that are too fragile to wear. Like any exquisite work of art, these can be mounted and displayed in lucite boxes or behind glass. This is probably true with any earrings from antiquity or earrings that are older, delicately constructed, or made by some of the more famous makers — in order for them to be preserved.

It takes sophisticated lab instruments and trained professionals to detect some of the more refined treatments. As technology improves, so do the treatments, which make them more and more difficult to detect. Any important gemstone should be accompanied by a lab report from a noted lab, such as GIA, AGL, HRD or AGS.

All treatments to a gemstone should be disclosed, since they could affect the stability and value of a stone. For instance, some treatments can break down if your earring is being worked on with a jeweler's torch or during a normal cleaning. It should be noted that some gemstones are routinely heat treated (as with sapphires) or oiled (as with emeralds). In these cases, it is important to know the amount and/or kind of treatment that a gemstone has had. In the case of routinely treated types of gemstones, the rare stone that is not treated can be especially valuable.

Technically, "hand-made" means using only hand tools. There are very fine pieces of jewelry that are "hand-made," but there are also pieces of fine-quality jewelry that involve using a combination of techniques. Many top-quality and one-of-a-kind pieces are custom cast (not considered "hand-made"), but are then hand-finished.

It is good to spend time perusing finer jewelry shops in a variety of locations to see styles and quality differences. There are high-quality antique jewelry shows in major cities across the country throughout the year. This is a particularly good way to learn about earrings because you can see the pieces up-close, look at the back, see how they are made, try them on, and ask questions.

HOW THEY FASTEN

The jeweler thinks of the means to fasten the earring as a "fitting" while jewelry catalogs describe the ready-made fastener as a "finding." When we go searching on the floor of our office or in the bed of our inamorata for the piece that came off our ear, we say, "Oh, I'm looking for the earring back." Or you don't call it anything, because you don't talk about it. I favor "closure," which is more from the wearer's point of view, but avoids the hesitation between "back" and "backing." "Closure" also has a whiff of elegance, rhyming with the French term for the same thing, "fermature," the same way that "tarte" is prettier if not more delicious than "pie."

Some fittings are invented at a point in time while others fall into disuse, but mostly once used they continue for hundreds or thousands of years. We order them here chronologically:

- **Ribbons or strings**: Inserted into the pierced hole, this was one way of wearing earrings in the Renaissance and they sometimes went over the earlobe, distributing the weight of more massive pairs.

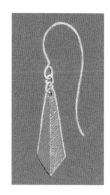

- **Shepherd's Crook**: Also called Swan's Neck, the curved hook goes through the ear and the ornament dangles at the other end. In French, this is known as the "le crochet" (general word for hook).

- **Hoops**: The ear wire can be at the top, side (boat earrings), or have a tube fitting where the ear wire goes into an incomplete tube. There are nifty variations on hoops from time immemorial until today: earwire at the top; loop at end of a hinge; continuous — here the post slides into the hollow hoop or a bead at the end of the hoop.

- **Kidney or French wire**: The ear wire is bent into a simple loop. By mid-Victorian times, this style closes by having the wire curve and form a hook catch. Another type of kidney wire has a dainty incomplete tube into which the earwire fits.

- **Accessory Ring**: Used for closure, it is a ring at the top of the wire that keeps the earring from slipping, and sometimes was threaded and attached to the hair for extra support. Used throughout the eighteenth century.

- **Poissardes**: These elegant ellipse-shaped earrings have an S-shaped support and threaded back to the front. The "S" holds the elongated hoop in place. Supposedly women who worked in the fish markets of Paris were the first to wear them, during the French Revolution, thus the name comes from the French for fishwife. Popular in the early 1800s.

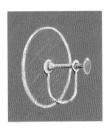

- **Screw back**: The finding was patented in 1894.

- **Threaded posts**: Like studs except the post has threads like a screw and has to be slid over them to fasten the earrings. Invented in the 1890s, its stud metal piece gradually grew thinner in diameter and had a friction nut. A variation known as the snap post has the post snap into a V-shaped latch at the back of the earring to secure it.

- **Clips**: Look, no holes! The clips have had numerous variations. In the 1940s and '50s, a two-part piece closed around the lobe, using mechanical pressure to hold them in place. Some are instruments of torture while others feel just fine. The finding was patented from 1934. Many variations of clips have appeared on the market and some had the stamp of the designer on the fitting.

- **Ear screws**: This unpleasant name describes the U-shaped earring that has a pad at the front and behind the lobe, and a threaded ear wire. When the mechanism is turned, the rear portion tightens on the ear.

- **Omega clips**: Post with clip back for added security; a hinged O-shaped lever behind the earring folds over the post to hold the earring in place. The omega-shaped wire that attaches to the ear gave this closure its name.

- **Post-and-clutch**: This style of stud is most popular today.

- **Huggies**: A hinge at the top releases the post; often the gemstones are channel-set.

- **Earcuffs**: A ring is pinched someplace on the ear, usually the top, with no need for piercing. The cuff fits on the rim of the ear.

- **Threaders**: Some shoulder duster earrings of one or more long strands of metal chain that thread through the piercing. Each side of the very fine chain hangs down from the ear and a metal post keeps it from falling out.

- **Lever-back**: This dainty hinge comes in two styles — back fastening and front fastening; that is, the earring goes through the earlobe back to front or front to back. The lever-back style dates from about 1880. One type of lever-back has a hook that passes through the lobe and is held in place by a hinge at the back of the earring. The curved end of the hole has to be very thin so as to go through the piercing. Another type has the hooked metal go from back to front, fastening in a bead of metal that is part of the design on the front of the ornament.

- **Post or Stud**: The closure of a single wire that juts out at the back of the earring was patented and introduced in the U.S. in 1871. It brings the decorative part of the earring right against the lobe. For some unaccountable reason, it was not used in ancient earrings of Egypt and the Mediterranean lands.

Sources

Abbé de Choisy. *The Transvestite Memoirs of the Abbé de Choisy*, trans. with an introduction by R.H.F. Scott. London, United Kingdom: Peter Owen, 1994.

Abbott, John S.C. *Hortense*. New York, New York: Harper & Bros., 1901.

Abrantes, Laure Junot. *At the Court of Napoleon: Memoirs of the Duchesse d'Abrantes*, ed. by Olivier Bernier. New York, New York: Doubleday, 1985.

Albersmeier, Sabine. *Bedazzled: 5000 Years of Jewelry – the Walters Art Museum*. London, England: D. Giles Ltd., 2006.

Algrant, Christine Pevitt. *Madame de Pompadour: Mistress of France*. New York, New York: Grove, 2003.

Ball, Joanne Dubbs. *Costume Jewelers: The Golden Age of Design*. Atglen, Pennsylvania: Schiffer Publishing, Ltd., 1997.

Bapst, G. *Histoire des Joyaux de la Couronne de France*. Paris, France: Hachette, 1889.

Barroll, John Leeds. *Anna of Denmark, Queen of England: A Cultural Biography*. Philadelphia, Pennsylvania: University of Pennsylvania Press, 2001.

Baumgarten, Linda. *What Clothes Reveal: The Language of Clothing in Colonial and Federal America*. New Haven, Connecticut: Yale University Press, 2012.

Becker, Vivienne. *Fabulous Costume Jewelry: History of Fantasy and Fashion*. Atglen, Pennsylvania: Schiffer Publishing, Ltd., 1993.

Bell, C. Jeanenne. *Answers to Questions about Old Jewelry 1840-1950*. Iola, Wisconsin: Krause, 2009.
How to be a Jewelry Detective. A.D., 2001.

Bernier, Olivier. *The Eighteenth-Century Woman*. New York, New York: Doubleday, 1982.
Louis XIV, A Royal Life. New York, New York: Doubleday, 1987.
The World in 1800. New York, New York: John Wiley & Sons, 2001.

Bresler, Fenton. *Napoleon III*. New York, New York: Carroll & Graf, 1999

Burrus, Christine. *Frida Kahlo: 'I paint my reality.'* London, England: Thames & Hudson, 2008.

Carbonel, Marie-Hélène and Javier Figuero. *La Véritable Histoire de la Belle Otero et de la Belle Epoque*. Paris, France: Fayard, 2003.

Castle, Charles. *La Belle Otero: The Last Great Courtesan*. Paris, France: M. Joseph, 1981.

Cera, Deanna Farneti and Jean Appleton. *Amazing Gems: An Illustrated Guide to the World's Most Dazzling Costume Jewelry*. New York, New York: Abrams, 1995.

Childers, Caroline. *Haute Jewelry: Prestigious Jewellery and Great Jewellers of the World*. New York, New York: Rizzoli, 1999.

Chrisman-Campbell, Kimberly. "Dressing to Impress: The Morning Toilette and the Fabrication of Femininity." *Paris: Life & Luxury in the 18th Century*. Los Angeles, California: J. Paul Getty Museum, 2011.

Cinamon, Diana Sanders. *Estate Jewelry 1760-1960*. Atglen, Pennsylvania: Schiffer Publishing, Ltd., 2009.

Corbett, Patricia. *Verdura: The Life and Work of a Master Jeweler*. New York, New York: Harry S. Abrams, 2002.

Cosgrave, Bronwyn. *Costume & Fashion: A Complete History*. London, England: Hamlyn, 2000.

Coss, Margery Cameron. *Victorian Jewellery*. London, England: Cassell, 1951.

d'Arfey, William. *Curious Relations*. New York, New York: William Sloane Associates, 1947.

Davis, Carolyn N. "Joseff of Hollywood." (www.guotbrothers.com).

Dawes, Ginny Redington with Olivia Collings. *Georgian Jewellery 1714-1830*. Suffolk, United Kingdom: Antique Collectors Club, 2007.

Dawes, Ginny Redington, Corinne Davidov, and Tom Dawes. *Victorian Jewellery: Unexplored Treasures*. New York, New York: Abbeville Press, 1991.

de Decker, Michel. *Diane de Poitiers*. Paris, France: Pygmalion, Gerard Watelets, 2004.

DeJean, Joan E. *The Essence of Style: How the French Invented High Fashion, Fine Food, Chic Cafes, Style, Sophistication and Glamour*. New York, New York: Free Press, 2005.

Dulong, Claude. *Marie Mancini*. Paris, France: Academique Perrin, 2002.

Dyson, C.C. *The Life of Marie-Amélie, Last Queen of France, 1782-1866*. New York, New York: D. Appleton, 1910.

Erlanger, Philippe. *Louis XIV*. London, England: Phoenix, 2003.

Ettinger, Roseann. *Popular Jewelry 1840-1940*. Atglen, Pennsylvania: Schiffer Publishing, Ltd., 2011.

Evans, Joan. *A History of Jewellery, 1100-1870*. Boston, Massachusetts: Boston Book and Art, 1970.

Fales, Martha Gandy. *Jewelry in America, 1600-1900*. Suffolk, United Kingdom: Antique Collectors' Club, 1995.

Filstrup, Chris and Jane. *Beadazzled: The Story of Beads*. New York, New York: Warne, 1982.

Filstrup, Jane Merrill. "Precious Platinum." *Town & Country*, June 1983.

Fleury, Maurice, (comte). *Louis XV Intime et les Petites Maîtresses*. Paris, France: Nabu Press, 2011.

Fontenay, Eugene. *Les Bijoux Anciens et Modernes*. Paris, France: Nabu, 2011; c. 1887.

Frasier, Antonia. *Love and Louis XIV: The Women in the Life of the Sun King*. New York, New York: Anchor, 2007.
Marie Antoinette: The Journey. New York, New York: Anchor, 2002.

Gallet, Danielle. *Madame de Pompadour ou le Pouvoir Féminin*. Paris, France: Librairie Arthème Fayard, 1985.

Gallet, Michel. *L'Epoque de Louis XVI*. Paris, France: Le Temps, 1964.

"Glass Blowing as a Fine Art." *Harper's Magazine*, vol. 42, February 1871; 337-54.

Goldemberg, Rose Leiman. *Antique Jewelry: A Practical & Passionate Guide*. Backinprint.com, 2000.

Goldsmith, Elizabeth C. and Dena Goodman. *Going Public: Women and Publishing in Early Modern France*. Ithaca, New York: Cornell University Press, 1995.

Goncourt, Edmond de. *Les Maîtresses de Louis XV: Lettres et Documents Inedits*. Paris, France: BiblioLife, 2009.

Goring, Elizabeth S. "Suffragette Jewellery in Britain." *Decorative Arts Society Journal* 26.

Grammet, Ivo. "Les Bijoux." *Splendeurs du Maroc*. Editions Plume/Musée Royal de l'Afrique Centrale, Tervuren, 1998.

Gregorietti, Guido. *Jewelry through the Ages*. New York, New York: American Heritage, 1969.

Guerber, Helene Adeline. *Empresses of France*. New York, New York: Dodd, Mead, 1901.

Haskell, Frances. *Rediscoveries in Art: Some Aspects of Taste, Fashion and Collecting in England and France*. London, England: Phaidon, 1980.

Haslip, Joan. *Madame de Barry: The Wages of Beauty*. New York, New York: Grove, 2002.

Herrera, Hayden. *Frida: A Biography of Frida Kahlo*. New York, New York: HarperCollins, 1983.

Hilton, Lisa. *Athenais: The Life of Louis XIV's Mistress – the Real Queen of France*. New York, New York: Little Brown, 2002.

Hinks, Peter. *19th Century Jewellery*. London, England: Faber and Faber, 1975.

Honour, Hugh. *Neo-Classicism, Style and Civilization*. New York, New York: Penguin, 1968.

Hughes, Diane Owen. "Distinguishing Signs: Ear-Rings, Jews and Franciscan Rhetoric in the Italian Renaissance City." *Past and Present 112*, 1986; 3-59.

Imbert de Saint-Amand and Arthur Léon (baron). *Louis-Napoleon et Mademoiselle de Montijo*. Paris, France: Dentu, 1897.

"Jewelry." *The Encyclopedia Britannica*, 11th Edition.

Joannis, Claudette. *Bijoux des deux Empires 1804-1870*. Paris, France: Somogy, 2004.

Jolly, Penny Howell. "Marked Difference: Earrings and 'The Other' in 15th-century Flemish Art." *Encountering Medieval Textiles and Dress: Objects, Texts, Images*, ed. by Desiree G. Koslin and Janet E. Snyder. New York, New York: Palgrave Macmillan, 2008.

Jones, Colin. *Madame de Pompadour: Images of a Mistress*. New Haven, Connecticut: National Gallery Publications with Yale University Press, 2002.

Klein, Richard. *Jewelry Talks: A Novel Thesis*. New York, New York: Vintage, 2002.

Koslovsky, Craig. *Evening's Empire: A History of Night in Early Modern Europe*. London, England: Cambridge University Press, 2011.

Legge, Edward. *The Empress Eugenie 1870-1910*. Whitefish, Montana: Kessinger, 2005.

Leinwand, Gerald. *1927: High Tide of the 1920s*. New York, New York: Basic Books, 2001.

Lester, Katherine, Oerke Morris, Bess Viola, and Helen Westermann. *Accessories of Dress: An Illustrated Encyclopedia*. New York, New York: Dover, 2004.

Lever, Evelyne, trans. by Catherine Temerson. *Madame*